BAKWA MAGAZINE

09

*Taxi Drivers
Who Drive Us Nowhere
and other Travel Stories*

Bakwa Magazine

EDITOR
Dzekashu MacViban

ASSISTANT EDITOR
Socrates Mbamalu

COPY EDITOR
Nfor E. Njinyoh
Kelechi Njoku

STAFF WRITER
Howard M-B Maximus

EDITORIAL ADVISER
Kangsen Feka Wakai

Bakwa Magazine is a project by Bakwa, a Cameroonian non-profit organisation that empowers creatives across various platforms.

Copyright © 2019 by Bakwa Magazine

The copyright of the stories in this issue remain with the individual authors.

Bakwa 09, October 28, 2019
ISBN: 978-1-7337526-1-9

Cover art: Yuliia Studzinska (via Dreamstime)
Cover design: Dante Besong

Contents

Taxi Drivers Who Drive Us Nowhere, *Howard Meh-Buh Maximus* 4

A Family History in a Passport, *Yovanka Paquete Perdigao* 13

The Africa We Get, *Kay Ugwuede* 30

Losing my passport to get home, *Munukayumbwa 'Mimi' Mwiya* 39

Prepare for Whiteness, *Sada Malumfashi* 45

Impossible n'est pas Camerounais, *Nkiacha Atemnkeng* 59

Vert le passeport, amers les aéroports, *Anne Marie Befoune* 79

Partir c'est mourir un peu, *Florian Ngimbis* 87

Maroua – Kousséri: No man's land!, *Raoul Djimeli* 99

Taxi Drivers

Who Drive Us Nowhere

Howard Meh-Buh Maximus

Taxi Drivers Who Drive Us Nowhere

Lagos, my friend says, is sick in both senses of the word; a city dealing with Dissociative Identity Disorder, with an emphasis on Dissociative. Its two main personalities—chaos and bliss, depend on what part of the city you find yourself. I laugh and ask him if he is talking about Douala. It is my second visit here; flying from Douala to Lagos to a deja-vu chaos standing solid on the street: bike riders slithering through impossible pinhole crevices, keke na peps overtaking any and every vehicle they can, and just across the road, bus drivers have parked their buses to fight. I once read on the internet that saying, "I live in Lagos and I missed an accident today" is tautology. Lagos is a potpourri of some Cameroonian cities—of chaotic Douala and serene Limbe, and something of Yaoundé, blended and dubbed; with Yoruba and Igbo replacing French, and different accents of English and Pidgin English. Like Douala, navigating the city by public transport is a chore at best. And while there are different degrees of this chore, my friend says his best bet, the car-less human that he is, is a taxi.

Taxis in Lagos are fancy. In Cameroon, they are all yellow, announcing their taxi-ness, except for the clandestine ones that transport people from one town to another. The first taxi I board in Lagos takes me from the Murtala Muhammed International airport, to a hotel in Oregun where I lodged. The driver's hair is kempt and he is fingering a fob which he wouldn't use. He compliments my luggage—the matching Ankara prints of my travel bag and backpack, before helping me lift them into the boot. He welcomes me to Nigeria with a smile that seems rehearsed before starting the trip.

My friend says he likes the white 2005 Toyota Corolla LE waiting for us outside. I tell him black is my colour when it comes to cars. The driver has been waiting for twelve minutes or so but he greets us politely and asks if he can start the trip. We thank him for waiting and ask him to take us to the bank. I am reminded of the Douala taxi driver; a vibrant late thirties-looking man who held us hostage in his car, asking us to pay an extra thousand for keeping him waiting ten minutes. We were hiring him to transport some equipment. Lagos is suffering a heatwave; the heat sticks to the skin like a bad nickname. I fan myself with a sheet of paper, waiting to turn into some kind of pastry from baking in the oven that was the car. The driver apologizes for the heat, tells me his AC had just stopped working, and I wonder if it is true. He apologizes so much that I stop counting after the third time. We are talking and he tells me he runs a Master's Degree program in Systems Engineering at the University of

Lagos. I am impressed, ask him how he manages school and driving a taxi. He tells me, declaratively, that this is Lagos; nobody owes you anything in Lagos, "you have to work for your bread," he says, and then insinuates that rich kids may not know this struggle. I tell him I am in Nigeria for a writer's residency program and he gushes, asks if I am not Nigerian. No, I tell him, I'm from Cameroon. He says *Oui oui*, confesses that is the only French he knows, laughs loudly and then says I could have fooled him—my complexion, my hair, I look Igbo. I laugh too, I have never thought of myself as someone who could be Igbo. He tells me his name is Femi, and as my friend approaches us, done with his transactions, as we prepare to leave the bank premises, the still smiling driver asks for my name and phone number. I give him, wondering if he will ever call.

It's been two months or so from the time I arrived Lagos—the undeniable hub of events. I am getting dressed now, preparing to go for one about sex and sexual health. It is happening at a highbrow restaurant on the island called The Backyard. The driver who takes me from Oshodi to The Backyard looks, in his T-shirt and jeans, like he is in his early twenties. He greets me when I get in and stays silent for the rest of the trip. A phone hangs from a holder attached to the windscreen, the map spread for both of us to see. I think of how functional this is, unlike with the drivers who kept glancing at the phone from their lap. It is dark and he is speeding on the highway, crossing red lights, overtaking anyone on his way. I think to make a joke about his telepathic knowledge of my hurriedness, but the grimace of concentration on his face leaves me silent. I watch him take turns as I try to follow up on the map like it was a video game. It is on this drive that I experience Lagos' bliss—speeding on an almost empty bridge, watching the city lights and water, listening to quiet afro-pop, the soundtrack to a trancy moviesque scene. It reminds me of Limbe, calm and breezy, and of the fact that if you asked a Limbe denizen what traffic is, they'd stutter at the question. In front of The Backyard, the driver shows me the tracker and we thank each other politely when I pay. It is the cheapest I have ever paid from the mainland to the island.

About a week later, my friend and I are on our way to the mall. Mr. Kunle, the elderly taxi driver, hates the Nigerian police. "The police is your friend my nyansh," he says and we laugh. He tells us hilarious stories of his police hate all the way to Ozone. He tells us about the different kinds of cars one would find on Lagos roads, tells us too about the girl who once got into his car with a big plastic bag containing weed; how the police had wanted to confiscate his car as if he was supposed to search passengers before carrying them; how they took all the money he had worked that day. We drive pass by some police officers and he grumbles an insult at them. We laugh. We are chatting and laughing so much he gets lost from not following the map on his lap. We see a handwritten banner that says *Repent and give your life to Christ for the judgment day is coming*. He agrees with the banner and preaches to us about the ills of fraud and fornication until he finds his way. I imagine he imagines us his children. At the mall, we tell him we are going to see a movie, and he parks his taxi and comes with us. He makes a joke about enjoying some of the money he works so hard to make. He lectures us on *Captain Marvel* as we walk in, and I am stunned that a man his age would know so much about American superhero movies like *Captain Marvel*. We go in to see the movie *Us* and he wants to find some amala to eat first. As we get our popcorn, I think of all the parents who toil so much making a living that they forget to live.

We once forget our keys in Solomon's black Camry and he drives all the way back to find us. The young Uni-Lag graduate, who quit his corporate job and has been driving a taxi for 3 years, tells us of the woman he had carried to Lekki, twice; a coincidence. And both times, she had insisted he come into her apartment. We would call him later, this driver with whom we discuss the pros and cons of social media, to give him a little thank-you token for returning our keys.

In Lagos, drivers of Ubers and Taxify are usually educated and rated by the passengers after every ride. It is a two-way street, as the drivers rate the passengers as well. There are consequences for bad reviews, and so everyone tries to be on their best behaviour. But it is not the case with Cameroon.

In Douala, a driver taking us to Akwa almost bumps into another car while trying to squeeze in an opening too small for his taxi. When we reprimand him, scared for our lives, he asks us to come sit behind the wheel if we think we are better drivers.

But true politeness is one that is not induced by the fear of receiving a poor rating. Like with Mr. T, who wears a tie, keeps his taxi sparkling, and welcomes all passengers with a smile, as if they just walked into his office. In Limbe, I sit in his taxi, so pleased that I refuse to take my balance, let it go as tip. There is also this driver I meet in Douala, whose name I do not ask. He tells me bits of his story. How he had been living and working in Bamenda before the Anglophone crisis started and he and his family had to run to Douala for refuge. He has lost his farms and

Taxi Drivers Who Drive Us Nowhere

now drives to support his family and find new schools for his children.

My friend says roads in Yaounde, in spite of the largeness of the city, are all interconnected. So one can take a taxi to anywhere standing on any side of the road. The problem is knowing where to stand to pay less. I have once paid triple the fare standing on the wrong side of the road, as the driver had to go round and round before arriving at my destination. Hiring taxis in Yaounde is different from hiring taxis in Lagos. In Lagos, you use an app; in Yaounde, you simply step out and find any empty taxi and tell them you are hiring. Sometimes, you just kick out the passengers already in the taxi before you hire it.

I'm in a hired taxi headed to Palais des Congrès for a movie award show in Yaounde. I am in a tailored blue suit; white espadrille and my pocket square is made from an Ankara print. I am feeling myself. The driver, a chatty elderly man looks at me as if sizing me up, before telling me the money I am proposing is not enough. I beg him, saying we are all hustlers in this country—he should forget the suit. He laughs, shakes his head and tells me he'll carry me because I look like his son. In the car, he complains about that same son he says I look like. Midway, he pauses, looks at me again and asks what is happening at the

Palais des Congrès that he had seen too many people going there this evening; was it a wedding? I think of explaining that it is a movie award show, one of the biggest in the country, but I worry that he will ask what that means, that he will ask if I am an actor, talk about the irresponsibility of young people in the entertainment industry. I worry that he will complain to the next passenger he carries about me, his son's look-alike, who was just as irresponsible as his son. I nod, and tell him, "Yes, it is a wedding. Me, and all the people you had seen before are going for a wedding."

When we get there, there are actors and actresses, TV presenters and guests, standing outside, in different shades of glam, different styles of dapper suits, designer agbadas, gowns that open at the back, right down to the waist, and then flow for meters like wedding dresses. He is looking at the scene, photographers with cameras, clicking on end, hosts with microphones interviewing guests as they walk in and I can see him trying to make sense of it all. I pay in a hurry and alight; from the window of the front passenger seat, before I leave and join the party, I explain to him that it is indeed a very fancy wedding.

A Family History

in a Passport

Yovanka Paquete Perdigao

In 1998 I was six years old when I arrived in plastic slippers in Lisbon. My grandmother Mamie grabbed me and my sister's hands so hard she left the imprint of her rings on our wrists. In the airport we were led to a queue where volunteers from Expo '98 were handing out little mascots of Gil, a plushie that looked like a dolphin in yellow shorts and a red shirt. "Bem-vindo a Portugal," said one of the volunteers as she handed me a doll. Outside, Tiozão was waiting for us. He was so tall I could barely distinguish his facial features; my head only reached his knees. But I could hear his roaring laughter as he showed us the way to the car. I peered out of the window in the backseat and saw Portugal with new eyes.

I had been born in Lisbon, which earned me the nickname of "alfacinha", the name given to the city's offspring. I had also visited Portugal a few times on summer vacation but had no real memories of what was supposed to be my country. My big sister had been born in France but had a Bissau-Guinean passport, so I was the true Portuguese person in the family, as my parents liked to tease. Naturally, when fall came and I was enrolled in primary school, I proudly proclaimed to the other children, many of whom had never seen a Black child in Queluz, that I was Portuguese. They were incredulous.

"But you are Black!"

"Black people are not Portuguese."

"White people are Portuguese."

"You are Black, so you can only be African!"

By the time my grandfather Papi showed up to collect me after school, I was deeply troubled. We walked back home without me uttering a word, just dragging my feet. Papi, as usual, was quiet himself until my mood persisted three more days. He asked what was wrong and I responded: "Who is my grandfather?"

Papi had a deep laugh like Tiozão.

"Me, of course!"

"But you are Black like the night and I am brown like the sundown."

Papi almost folded himself from more laughter. I was even more confused. If the kids at school were right, this man I had loved so deeply couldn't be my grandfather. If you had to be one colour to belong somewhere, then why was Papi black like the night and the rest of us brown like sundown? I explained my childish logic and he patted me on the head.

"Humans come in all colours," he said. "It's like painting. You take white pink like Mamie and mix it with black night and a tinge of yellow, and it becomes brown like your Maman and Papa. Since they are both brown, they made brown babies."

It made sense, although white pink and black night did not make brown, but I didn't tell him that. Suddenly a weight was lifted from my heart. Papi was my grandfather after all! But, wait a minute, if he was right about colours then I was still Portuguese.

"Papi, eu sou Portuguesa?"

"Sim claro, nasceste aqui."

"But at school they said I am not. I have to be White to be Portuguese."

"That's because they don't know, they don't understand."

That day I went straight to those children who had stripped me of my nationality and told them I was Portuguese. They scoffed but I persisted by explaining my grandfather's analogy of colours: I was brown because I had Black night and White pink. They didn't get it but since I was the tallest child in my classroom, they didn't dare to challenge me, and for the rest of primary school, no one dared tell me I was not Portuguese.

B

Years later, I carried my little red Portuguese passport, travelling at ease with no regard to others without that privilege. I never knew any other life until my sister told me about the constant paperwork our Mamie had to fill for benefits while we lived in Lisbon.

"What benefits?"

"Don't you remember the table always covered with forms? Mamie was always filling them up to get money to take care of us, but it was always hard because we were not Portuguese citizens."

"I was not Portuguese?"

"Yeah, dummy. We came here with a Bissau-Guinean passport. What did you think?"

Naturally, at six years old, I had not been preoccupied with passports, visas or renewing documents, and when I was old enough to be responsible, I travelled with the famous red passport. So I had assumed, all these years, that I was born Portuguese and had been a citizen of Portugal with its "rightful" passport.

"But I was born there, Maman always joked I was an alfacinha!"

I was just finding out that Portugal operated a jus sanguinis law: my grandparents and parents were Bissau-Guineans; my birth in Lisbon had not granted me Portuguese citizenship. The process by which I had found myself travelling the world *carefree* had been a deliberate, exhausting, and humiliating ordeal, leading to the question I had posed years ago to my Papi. I had grown up thinking of myself as exclusively Black, because in Portugal I was always thought of as the African girl. I also had no white family on the other side, no white grandparents, or white uncles and aunts, or white cousins to compare. My family was an array of colours ranging from pearly to mahogany, to indigo blue, but we all called ourselves Black. Mamie who had Black Indian hair and porcelain skin, and thus was often mistaken for Lebanese, never even considered claiming her father's whiteness. On the other side, my father's father had curly hair and a nose that was Portuguese aristocracy. And in my father's family, every generation carried a boy named Francisco or Macario, the legacy of the two Portuguese brothers who had come to make fortunes in the colonies and left a Black family.

It was in our blood, Portugal's colonial legacy but also Africa's screams. It marked us different from both sides and made us a family that could never settle anywhere. My family had been always the first to embrace change. We were never patriotic, except for my father who had given his best years to Guinea-Bissau. My mother's side had always been an odd mix of foreigners, from Goa to Cape Verde, from São Tomé and

Príncipe to Guinea-Bissau. The intersection of the -isms—imperialism, colonialism, racism—meant that one had to always be ready to become something else. Like my Indian ancestor, Damasceno, who had ended up in Guinea-Bissau studying the tsetse fly. The Portuguese had found it tedious to send their own white doctors to African colonies, so they figured they could train Indians in Goa and ship them to Africa. Damasceno was groomed to serve the Portuguese Empire in Mozambique and Cape Verde, and he settled in Guinea-Bissau. He later disappeared. Some say he found his way back home, but not before leaving a baby boy Pedro behind.

My grandfather had a slightly different story: his mother forced him to leave São Tomé at the age of twelve to be a tailor in Guinea-Bissau. A massacre orchestrated by the Portuguese, which killed thousands and left the waters around the island crimson, had put the fear of God in my grandfather's mother; she was sure that one day the Portuguese would be back to slaughter more innocents, so she told my grandfather to run and never look back. He didn't until he met his wife Guida, the love child of a naval officer and Indian-Guinean girl.

Fausto Bogalho had met my great-grandmother Mariana in Bissau and they conceived Guida. Fausto returned to his already established family in Lisbon, leaving young Mariana pregnant and poor. All the money her ancestors who once came from Goa and Cape Verde had had been squandered on gambling, so Mariana pulled up her sleeves and raised a mixed-race baby in a country trying to liberate itself from Portuguese oppression. Guida never met her father, only saw him once at eighteen, and a few months later he was dead. She had only one picture of him and she was twirling it between her fingers, thinking of the irony she found herself in, sitting in her kitchen tile in Lisbon. She had vowed to never ask anything of that Portuguese side of hers, yet she knew that if she didn't dial her White half-brothers' number, she would regret it one day. Guida had to decide to take the Portuguese nationality to protect her family. It was the early 2000s and Europe was turning to multiculturalism, but Guida knew it was not for long. She had worked long enough in the colonial administration to know that. The Tugas could only stand Black people long enough to leave a trail of mulattos. War was also still raging in Guinea-Bissau, making home a distant dream. Guida's husband squeezed her shoulders and she finally dialled her White half-brothers' phone.

Guida and two of her half-brothers went to the civil register where they declared her to be their father's child born in

A Family History in a Passport

Guinea-Bissau during his colonial service. Guida got her Portuguese passport and passed her citizenship to her husband and three children.

For my father, it was simpler. It was well known that the Perdigão family in Guinea-Bissau was from an aristocratic family from Coimbra. Little was known of the two offspring of an influential judge except that they had not pursued the more respectful way of living having set out to the colonies. Macario and Francisco "married" local women and their descendants became influential mestiços living in lavish homes in colonial Bolama. My grandfather had been born witnessing the last remnants of this luxury but had held on to the documents that proved his jus sanguinis status. He passed it quickly to his twelve children except my father Caio. My grandfather believed my father was to be the next great Bissau-Guinean politician to walk in the footsteps of Amilcar Cabral, so Caio was groomed to take that path and was spared Portuguese nationality.

That was until the 1998 civil war made our family refugees in Lisbon. This was why my grandma was filling out forms for benefits for her two granddaughters who were Bissau-Guinean citizens and not worthy of any assistance in Portugal. My father went down to the civil registrar where he had been left out as a child of his father, to prove he was indeed his son and thus eligible for Portuguese nationality. He passed it to my mother, my sister and me.

※

This is how I became the holder of the red passport that opened doors anywhere in the world.

I was twenty-six years old when I became aware of the burden of travelling with an African passport. Twenty-six years of being blissfully ignorant and privileged thanks to the complex imperialist forces that had brought colonialism and slavery into my blood. I had travelled back and forth between Europe and Africa without the hassle of visas, travelled the African continent and been greeted with enthusiasm and no suspicion.

But if my short life was one of privileged travel, there was never a time White people let me forget that I was "lucky" to possess these documents. Just like when I was six years old in the playground, I realized I was always going to be an anomaly to my Portuguese White peers. As a Black person with a Portuguese passport, it guaranteed my access to privilege but came with conditions. Every single time I had to renew my passport, my family and I were the subject of ignorant and racist remarks. When we went to renew my little sister's passport, we were baby-talking in French and one of the attendants rolled her eyes and said: "They give nationality to anyone these days, even those who don't speak Portuguese."

My other sister and her husband had gone to register her child at the Portuguese embassy in London and were served with outlandish interpretations of the law that shifted every time she protested.

"Some people have clearly been living far away for too long they don't even know their country's laws," the man behind the glass spat out in disdain.

Renewing our documents was always a complicated, tiring, humiliating experience we underwent because we knew too well the power of that passport.

But, to me, it also became a game. I always identified as Black, the first thing I had been called in my so-called mother country, but I loved parading my passport in front of White Portuguese people. I would serve my best Portuguese interspersed with French and English, delighting in their horror, throwing them off. I would remind them I was born in the famous Francisco de Xavier hospital, right at the centre of Lisbon, in one of its most affluent neighbourhoods, just to irritate them even more. I walked with the confidence of an

Angolan entering a Cartier store in downtown Baixa, just to smirk in their faces. I was just like them, Portuguese but Black. It was perhaps important to me at that time because I knew instinctively that not having that passport was the gateway to being dehumanised. Portugal's colonial past is often seen as a technicolour Tropicalia dream, with well-intentioned Whites, mulatto babies, invisible-yet-there Black people smiling and samba music in the background. After all, it was the Brazilian sociologist Gilberto Freyre that had argued that the Portuguese were better colonisers than other European nations. The warmer climate and rich history of the Celts, Romans, Visigoths and Moors had made the Portuguese more humane colonisers. A despicable lie that other Africans repeated when they found out I was from Lusophone Africa. A lie my grandfather had felt kneeling in glass shards for days for daring to dream of independence. He walked touching the walls, a habit he picked up from being thrown in jail and talking to the walls. It was only three years but it had consequences that went beyond and touched even those that were yet to be born. And there were other families, others who had even stayed decades, others who had lost their sense of self, others that had self-destructed. In the bush, others were faring just as bad. The same weapons of

A Family History in a Passport

destruction used in Vietnam were being deployed against those who had run to join the guerrillas of the PAIGC, napalm, and defoliants. Eyes, legs, arms, whole bodies dancing in a frenzied way. Old and young, man and woman, they were all dying, killed by the very "humane" Portuguese forces. We thought it was over when independence came, but a lot of us found ourselves with one foot in Africa and another in Portugal. The mother country could never be home, no matter how much you tried, but the passport was the only thing that saved you from being desecrated in the ghettos of Lisbon. I did not know the struggle of other Africans, but I knew what that passport was keeping me from in Portugal.

Years later, my mother said it was time we renewed our Bissau-Guinean passports.

I raised my eyebrows at that suggestion.

"Why?"

"What do you mean why?"

"You've never even taken us back."

"You know exactly why, it wasn't safe."

"What's the point of having that passport when you have not been back in almost fifteen years and don't speak the language? You almost forbade us to speak Crioulo!"

"Yovanka, really? When did I forbid you guys?"

I shrugged. It wasn't that I did not want the Bissau-Guinean passport, but I saw no use having a document to link me to a country that had chased me out in plastic slippers. It was also the same place that had fractured my family and engulfed so many others. I wanted to go back but I also didn't want to go back, and I didn't need a reminder of this contradiction.

"Maybe your Dad and I wanted you guys to grow away from Bissau, because we were afraid. I almost lost you, your sister, your father, my parents, my brother and so many more people," my mother said, her hands trembling a bit, and I felt her fear. She had been in America when the war started, screaming down the telephone for my father to find a way to get us out.

So we went to the embassy of Guinea-Bissau in Senegal. Even stepping there with so many curious faces brought me a bit of anxiety. To start with, I did not speak Crioulo but my last name would not let me pass for nothing else than a Bissau-Guinean. The lady behind the counter looked at my documents and promptly asked, "Your name? Is your father in politics?"

A Family History in a Passport

"No," I answered. I sensed it was a trick question coming, to suss whose child I was, but I was grateful she didn't ask more. Guinea-Bissau is a country so small that everyone knows each other, and almost very likely, everyone is related. My own parents met as flower boy and flower girl at a wedding of two family acquaintances. The first question people from Guinea-Bissau always ask is, "Your last name?" followed by "Who are your parents?" and—boom!—they know right away your whole family history.

The lady made me take a picture and sign. I was to return the following week to collect the passport, which was never used. There was no much point, as using it would have meant visas and questions, and with Guinea-Bissau being touted as a Narco-state, I was going to risk having immigration asking me if I was transporting drugs—a joke overplayed at school that got tiring to the point of tears. The passport stayed pristinely the same until it expired and I still never went back to Guinea-Bissau. It did make me feel more legitimately Bissau-Guinean though, even as its blank pages reminded me firmly of my self-imposed exile. There was always a good reason not to go back, another coup, finances, university exams, even though I travelled frequently to see my parents in neighbouring Senegal.

B

Finally, my sister thought it would be a good idea to start a PhD with our country as a subject, and so she had to go back. As the younger sister, I followed her on a second trip, with my father. I got a visa on arrival with my Portuguese passport, and I was back eighteen years later. It was very simple after all.

 I spent two weeks going back to old places like our first home, our grandparents' house, our church, the square we went to on Saturdays, the shawarma place. At every turn there was a familiar face but I couldn't remember from where, even though they remembered me and marvelled at how big my sister and I had gotten. It was the end of a chapter but I realized as we were leaving that nothing had really changed. I had come back thinking that a huge part of myself was going to be healed or that I would suddenly feel a surge of love and longing to stay, but none of that happened. With an African passport or not, I had never stopped "feeling African". I might have had Portuguese nationality for most of my life, but I always felt like a tourist in Portugal yearning to go back to the African continent. Like brother Chullage rapped, "Koração lá e korpo ká em Pretugal[1]". As we drove through the countryside, I marvelled at the sun setting in the green hills and felt at ease despite the eighteen-year lapse. I left with my Portuguese passport, but I was still African—maybe just one whose ancestors had sacrificed so much for the privilege of travelling without borders. I am reminded of this every time the White man at the counter of the airport still raises his eyebrows at me.

"O seupassaporte? Portuguesa?" he asks.

"Portuguesa sim," I say, and smile sweetly.

---

[1] Rap lyric by Portuguese rapper from Cape Verdian parents, Chullage, from his album "Rapensar". It translates to "Heart there and body here in Pretugal". Pretugal is the anagram for the word Preto [Black] and Portugal [Portugal]

The Africa We Get

Kay Ugwuede

The streets of Yaoundé are very much like Lagos—alive, fraught with bright yellow cabs and roadside vendors offering a variety of merchandise, from sneakers to roasted groundnuts generously coated in sugar. At night, along the adjoining road to the street where our rented apartment is hidden, makeshift food stalls emerge next to each other, filling the air with the aroma of grilled meat and vinegar mixed with mayonnaise. The evening's soundtrack is distinct: a symphony of car horns, revving engines, and muffled music from Le Quebec, a busy nightclub that concentrates activity at the junction leading into the quiet street where we are spending a few days working and planning our next stop. I am in Yaoundé with a team of five artists and a project manager. We are travelling, or attempting to travel, to Maputo, Mozambique, from Lagos, Nigeria, through seven countries, by road. This is the first leg of the trip. Organised by the Invisible Borders Trans-African Photography Organisation, the road trip project is in its ninth year. It is my first time outside Nigeria.

I first learnt about the Invisible Borders road trips in 2017. At the time, they were about to begin the second leg of a trip across Nigeria, questioning the country's colonial cartography and how the country has negotiated its unity since the exit of her colonisers. I thought the idea was audacious. And timely.

I have heard it said that it is easier for an American to travel the continent than for an African to do same. But even travelling outside the continent as an African does not come as effortlessly as it is usually presented, especially on social media. Not many document the frantic search for appointment openings, the application forms and stack of documents you have to prepare, the nerve-racking interviews, or the lengthy waits at the embassies and consulates. In the high-resolution images of blue beaches and endless skies, there are no motifs symbolising "the curse of the green passport" or border laws that portend more singling out at airports, more scrutiny, more meaningless rejections. While stringent access requirements for Africans to travel within Africa have relaxed over the years, travelling within the continent as an African remains a nightmare, one I was to experience first-hand.

B

Our trip begins on a clear-skied Thursday in October, with courtesy calls to Kelechi Amadi-Obi and Uche James-Iroha, both legendary photographers, and the latter one of the road trip project's pioneer participants. Two days later, we are headed to Enugu, my hometown, from where we head to Ikom and prepare to exit Nigeria through the Cameroon border, the first we would encounter on the road. Having originally been selected as a guest participant from Nigeria, my journey was to end at Ikom, but an impromptu exit of one of the trans-border participants opens up an opportunity for me, one I accept without hesitation. We are heading eastwards towards central Africa, first into Cameroon from Bamenda, through its administrative capital, then an audacious attempt to the Central African Republic, exiting into the Democratic Republic of Congo, before berthing in Rwanda. From Lagos to Enugu, we are accompanied by long stretches of vegetation, unmotorable roads, and occasional police checkpoints. Until we get to Ikom. By the next day after our arrival in Ikom, every person we have had the chance to meet and explain to the vision of our project, including our next travel itinerary has the same piece of advice: we cannot cross into Cameroon from Ikom. To ascertain the veracity of their claims before making huge logistic changes to the travel plan, we spend a few days at the border talking to business owners, merchants, people criss-crossing the border for trade and love. We even visit a camp settlement in Ogoja housing thousands of Cameroonians fleeing Bamenda as a result of a divisional crisis, much like Nigeria's Biafran resurgence which has been ongoing since late 2017. Bamenda, being the seat of Cameroon's political opposition party Front Social-Démocratique, and its "secessionist capital", is at the centre of this conflict. Alongside the separatist crisis, the fate of Paul Biya, Cameroon's remote-working eighty-five-year-old president who has been in power since the 1980s is also hanging in the balance albeit theoretically, considering how democracy plays out in most parts of the continent. His victory or loss at the polls, going by the conversations we have at the displaced persons camp, would determine what becomes of our movement across the border safely and freely. With a travel itinerary in hand and very limited time, we cannot wait for the outcome of the election.

So, to get into Yaoundé, Cameroon's inland capital, within forty-eight hours, we travel fifteen hours from Ikom, east of Nigeria; up north to Yola; three hours from Yola to Limané, speedboating across River Benue, with a stopover at Barnaké to stamp our passports; another four hours to Garoua; and six more to Ngaoundere to break a seventeen-hour journey to Yaoundé, all the while hauling boxes of filming gear, office supplies, reference books, personal belongings, and the sharpest versions of our minds.

ℬ

My re-education of travelling across Africa's borders as an African are already underway and continues at Barnaké, an outpost immigration office on the outskirts of Cameroon. The official who greets us is an elderly man with a thin frame and long limbs. His face is unwelcoming, as though he has been stirred from a nap. When we present our green passports, a conversation ensues in French with the only French speaker amongst us. He wants our visas, or at least a laissez-passer into Cameroon. None of us, save the young half-Cameroonian guiding us into the country, has either document. We do not need one. Nigeria and Cameroon have an agreement that does not require any such document for entry for a period of up to 90 days. The official seems flustered when we explain this to him. I am surprised at his lack of knowledge about the laws guiding the border he guards. After a moderately short wait spent trying to convince him of the legitimacy of our entry, he stamps our passports begrudgingly, and we continue on our way.

Our next hitch would come with our next border crossing from Cameroon into DR Congo. After crossing the Central African Republic off our list of destinations due to security concerns, the Democratic Republic of Congo is our next port of call with a trip planned from Zongo to Lisala, the capital of the

Mongala Province in the country's north-west region; to Kisangani; and ending in Bukavu. We are to fly into DR Congo from Cameroon and continue by road from Bukavu to Kigali. Except that to enter DR Congo, we would need to purchase return tickets that assured the authorities that we would leave just as we had come in. The average cost of return tickets from Yaoundé or Douala, Cameroon's more commercial capital, to Kinshasa can begin anywhere from $1,100 upwards, a cost that had not been factored into our *road* trip budget. To get a visa into DR Congo with your green passport could cost as high as $340— double this amount if you are looking to speed things up. A Schengen Visa into Europe costs just about $70. A US visa costs anything from $160 to $205, depending on which visa type you require.

With our original entry route into DR Congo botched, a RwandAir flight takes us from Douala to Kigali, from where we drive through the most beautiful landscape to Goma, a border town in eastern DR Congo and capital of the North Kivu province. While on the flight to Kigali, I come across the African Union's Agenda 2063 with the tagline, "The Africa We Want", tucked into the magazine compartment of the seat in front of me. One of its agenda points promises an all-access passport that will encourage freer exchange of knowledge and resources and drive the continent towards growth.

The deadline for the AU's goals is still forty-four years away.

According to a 2018 African Visa Openness Index, Africans require visas to travel to more than half the countries on the continent, making travel around Africa much easier for an American than an African. Whether as a result of political instability, astronomic fares or bureaucracies, these borders governments across the continent guard so jealously are not, interestingly, demarcations of our own making but imperialist cartographies that resulted from the dividing of Africa at the Berlin Conference in 1884. Its sole aim was to enrich the imperialists and took no cognizance of the diversity that existed on the continent—and still does. And so, while African states, from the 1950s, began to regain their pseudo-independence, these borders remained irrevocable vestiges of the looting and subduing of the continent, which African leaders continue to perpetuate by making the continent's countries inaccessible.

The African Union's response to the intercontinental travel challenges of Africans has come in the form of an all-access border pass, and though this may seem like a clear-cut solution to easing travel within the continent, it is only a part of an intricately woven web of challenges. Exorbitant visa fees, airways that are indirectly linked, unclear and tit-for-tat border laws are all part of this complex problem that turn borders into impenetrable vaults for Africa's daughters and sons. Agreeably, a number of these concerns are captured in the AU's 2063 Agenda, but, for me, the thought that the deadline for their accomplishment has been set forty-five years from now is disconcerting and surely a far cry not only from the Africa we desire but also the one we *need* if we consider the results and gifts that a borderless continent will bring.

Losing my passport to get home

Munukayumbwa 'Mimi' Mwiya

Ninety is the maximum number of days you can stay in most African countries as a tourist, visa-free or not. At the end of May 2017 I travelled to Nigeria on a thirty-day tourist visa. I stayed two hundred and twenty-two days, without having to renew my visa or officially extend my stay. Yes, I was an illegal immigrant. I didn't have a plan for that trip besides my desire to live in Nigeria indefinitely, customs and consequences be damned.

My plan didn't work out, though, and I eventually had to think about coming back home, which, of course, wouldn't be too easy a feat, having overstayed by over six months. I hadn't thought to change the dates on my return ticket, so, for starters, I needed money for a ticket back. I also needed money to pay the fine because I would be fined for overstaying.

I talked to a friend about my predicament, and she said she would talk to someone at immigration about what my options were. Her feedback was, there is a fixed fine of two thousand, five hundred US dollars, so I could pay that; or I could leave Nigeria through the border with Benin. Someone at the border could easily be bribed to stamp me out of the country. I liked the idea. I would get to visit a new country; I love to travel. Benin is on the list of countries Namibians can travel to visa-free. But I know no one in Benin, so I wasn't sure I wanted to travel there for the first time under my circumstances.

The immigrations contact mentioned something else: he didn't know about other countries, but he knew that most Nigerians, when they overstayed anywhere, often just went to the Nigerian Embassy to report their passports lost, then applied for emergency travel documents. It works because no one ever checks when your entry date was or when your departure date should have been if you aren't using the passport you got into the country with. Ahn-ahn! Truly, Nigerians make me happy!

But I kept that option in the back of my mind; I wasn't sure I had the guts to do it. I was exploring other options, talking to all my Nigerian contacts, asking them to talk to all their contacts, to see how I could leave the country without paying the hefty fine. One of the contacts told me that if I flew from Abuja, instead of Lagos where I was, he could find someone who would help me get out for five hundred dollars. Personally, I was ready to continue my illegal immigrant ways in Nigeria. I had a roof over my head, rent-free, because Nigerians are nice people, and I was volunteering at a place that gave me transport fare and lunch. I was content. But there were people who wanted me back home. One of them was my big brother who had financed the larger part of my trip. I told him how much the fine was and how much I could get it down to if I left from Abuja. He spoke to his own Nigerian contacts and one of them told him, "Bros, Nigerians are always staying longer than their visas allow, all over the world, and they just go to the embassy to report their passports lost. Just tell your sister to go to the Namibian Embassy and say she lost her passport." This was a thing o!

The Namibian embassy is in Abuja. So, around Christmas, I quickly made plans to travel to Abuja. I found the embassy had closed for the holidays, and I had to wait until the New Year to go there. I used the time before then to reconnect with old friends, make new ones, and go to the police to declare my passport lost. In Namibia, when you want a police declaration, you walk into the police station, make your declaration, and walk out. The most trouble you will have is having to correct the horrible grammar and spelling of the police officers writing the declaration.

In Nigeria, I had to visit three different offices and pay a couple thousand naira—heu! One of numerous reminders of how easy we have things in Namibia.

I got my declaration and anxiously waited for the embassy to resume business. I went to tell my lies and was nearly caught in them because the man issuing the ETDs seemed to enjoy his job a little too much and actually wanted to call the Home Affairs head office in Windhoek to check things like, what trips had been made on my passport before I 'lost' it—ahn-ahn! Fortunately for me, Namibia's Home Affairs employees don't take their jobs so seriously; getting hold of anyone in the office he was trying to call was near impossible.

After a couple of hours, and for a small fee, I had my ETD. The next day I went to buy my ticket, and the day after that, I was on my way home. Just like that! Going through the airport was a breeze; only one female security guard asked me what had happened to my passport, but even she seemed to just be asking for small talk's sake.

I am not proud that I cheated the system, but I continue to be baffled by how hard African travel systems are on Africans. I've long given up on us ever getting the "African passport" the AU promised us years ago, but I wish they would at least give us something that makes travelling and living in each other's countries a little easier. Something like the Schengen visa. I would never risk staying past my visa validity in a European country because Europe is not my backyard and the muzungus scare me. But with a Schengen visa, I would also never have much trouble travelling from one European country to another. It's as though each of the Schengen states have a pact where they agreed that if one country has okayed a traveller, they trust the judgment of that country. And I'm pretty sure most Europeans can come and go as they please within EU member states. The EU could teach the AU a thing or two about what it means to be a continental union, but that's a story for another day.

Prepare for Whiteness

Sada Malumfashi

i.

We are in a cocoon of unventilated air, breathing in the same oxygen and circulating the same carbon dioxide. This is the boarding area of the Nnamdi Azikiwe International Airport in Abuja, a prison cell of sorts, but my first gateway to Europe. We are all humans crammed into the area, ready to be transported out of Nigeria, out of Africa, to Germany, France, and the United States. We are sweating black bodies, our shoulders are puffed with pride. We are privileged, flying away from the motherland to a destination and journey other black bodies once dreaded. The few white bodies here are not shoulder-puffed but relieved, eager to flee the sweltering heat.

It is midnight when the Lufthansa flight lifts us into the Abuja skies. I lean into my seat and select *Avengers: Infinity War* on the movie screen. But soon I am sleeping, and this sleep holds a myriad of dreams: I am plunging into a well, the plane is a bottle, and I am an ant being tossed around in it. Then Thanos appears on a screen, snapping his fingers, and screaming at me.

I wake up to clicks of seat belts and a view of Frankfurt's skies.

ii.

The Frankfurt Airport is a race to meet connecting flights. I follow signposts—and there are lots of them here. I am in a rush. Change of altitude. Change of language. Change of culture.

The entry to Europe at Frankfurt is like the gates to heaven. Those with good deeds, the righteous ones in the eyes of the immigration Gods, would be the ones queuing in front of a sign that says, "EU Passport". Their queue moves quickly, and they are soon given a pass to heaven. Two steps away is another queue: the one for non-EU passports. This does not necessarily mean you are bad, or a sinner. It is just that you are not guaranteed passage to heaven until you answer certain questions.

An officer with neatly arranged hair, suited in a crisp turquoise uniform and matching tie, spits questions at me in accented English as she shuffles through my documents.

"Where are you heading to? Final destination?"

"Sylt."

"The island?"

"Yes." Each one-word answer comes through with a measured smile.

"What for?"

"A writing residency."

"Writing?"

"Yes. I'm a writer."

"Oh! So, what are you writing about?"

"I am supposed to write a novel."

"Can you tell me about the novel?"

"If I do I'll have to kill you."

The line came out wrong. She misses the sarcasm. There is no smile on her face anymore. The stamp in her hand hangs in the air. My entry to heaven is being contemplated.

"There will be a beautiful German character like you in it though," I add, baring my teeth at her, pleading.

The smile is returning. A brief laughter. The stamp drops down.

ℬ

When I was a child my favourite class in Islamic School was on Wednesdays, the last day of the Islamic week, with Thursdays and Fridays being weekends. At Islamic School, we sat cross-legged on praying mats—the boys in white jallabiyas, the girls in coloured hijabs—and listened to the sira of the prophets and other historical forms narrated by the mallam in beautiful stories. I fell in love with Wednesdays because of the stories: there were no admonitions, threats, punishments, or constant preaching happening on such days—just beautiful storytelling. And one of the stories I loved had descriptions of Jannah, heaven, with its eight principal gates, where angels salute all those who pass through. Whether these gates of heaven are metaphorical or literal, the stories left an imprint of their beauty on my childhood. Heaven was described as filled with material delights—great food, flowing springs, wells of honey and milk. In there, there is no hurt, sorrow, fear or shame. Anything you want and long for is in Jannah. But only the righteous, those with good deeds, find their final abode in the garden.

B

It is only the first light of dawn. My passage from Frankfurt to Hamburg is through gate A11, a path through a sea of chaos. I arrive at the boarding gate in the nick of time, dragging my baggage trolleys. The hostess at the gate smiles.

"Hamburg? Lufthansa?"

"Yes," the hostess says. "Please have a seat. It is a few minutes to time."

In a few minutes she speaks into the microphone on her desk and begins the pre-boarding announcement. First class passengers, nursing mothers, the disabled and elderly are invited to board first. Regular boarding for us who are abled, economy class, not old enough, and not nursing babies will begin in about ten minutes.

Each passenger places their boarding pass on a barcode scanner and is permitted entry into the gate. I am observing and learning, and soon it is my turn. I place my boarding pass on the scanner. The automated barcode entry gate does not open. I try again. And again. No green pass. I step aside and signal to the hostess about my predicament, with a tinge of embarrassment. She collects my boarding pass, looks at it, and says with a smirk, "Ah, Nigeria." She types something into the computer, and signals me to pass.

iii.

Hamburg is my final gate to heaven. My luggage will take forever to arrive. I keep shuttling between belts 6 and 7, waiting to spot my luggage in either one of them.

Then my bags pop out and I sigh. But there is no relief as Hamburg is yet another race—this time to find trains. There is a woman near me speaking rapid Yoruba to a man. The woman is fiery, but easier to approach than the blank white faces strutting past and waiting for their luggage; she is motherly. She walks me to the exit that leads to the trains. I ride an elevator from the baggage claim exit, and just below, under the airport, there is a train town: so many different platforms, so many trains. I check my email and find the instructions I'm looking for.

I will send your train ticket. Please print out or use on your mobile device. These are possible connections for you: Hamburg Airport – departs 09:53.

It is 9:50. I look up. There are two trains facing me. I continue reading the instructions.

Platform 3 Train type: S1.

A train begins to move. Have I missed it? My eyes pop at a sign: Platform 3. The train is stationary. I run to it. I jump in and it begins to move. I hope that I am not on the wrong train. It had moved at exactly 9:53—German efficiency. It had to be the right one.

The view of Hamburg from the train is a delight. Graffiti and bawdy human-sized paintings on all walls outside the train tracks. Hamburg is classy, sexy, and inviting. Music resonates from inside the train. There is a beggar—a white beggar—playing a trumpet and walking down the aisle, a cup in his hand. I am tempted, out of habit, to pull out a ten-euro note from my wallet and dash him for his art, but my brain does a quick conversion of that to naira, and I dash him a warm smile instead.

The train has a stop at Hamburg-Altona station where I would be required to change trains and platforms.

Hamburg-Altona – departs 10:40

Platform 7, train type: RE6

We arrive at 10:31. I cannot see platform 7 here. I cannot see Train RE6. I have nine minutes. I use two minutes to walk back and forth to nowhere exactly. You are always disoriented when you are in a race with time. I use another two minutes to find a comfortable face to ask questions and another one minute to keep relaying messages across English and German and playing along with sign language and shouting, *Sylt, the Island*, at the top of my voice. But it doesn't matter how high you raise your voice in English; the high pitch does not convey your message in German. I use another one minute to decipher the platforms and realize that they are actually above me. The escalator ride upwards takes about one minute, and the station appears above as a bazaar of sorts: bigger trains, multiple tracks. It takes me another minute to adjust to the new surroundings, and yet another one to find Train RE6 on platform 7.

As I run to the platform, the train is already moving. A voice says from behind me, weirdly in pidgin, "Sylt, ba? E don go. Another one in one hour time ehn." She is another motherly figure, fully kitted in jackets. Now she wheels her trolley away. I realize I am finally out of buildings and trains and in the open skies of Europe for the first time. The cold wind sends chills into my scalp. I run into a sheltered coffee house and scavenge in my hand luggage for winter clothing.

ℬ

Train RE6 to Westerland will take me across a causeway from mainland Germany to the island of Sylt. I settle down for a ride of about four hours. The pidgin-speaking woman from earlier comes into the coach and I greet and thank her for her help. She is with two other people now, a young man and an older one. She asks where I am from and answers herself. "Nigeria eh?"

I nod.

"But where in Nigeria?"

"Kaduna."

"Ah." She says I am not the typical Nigerian you find in Germany—the ones from the southern part of the country.

Her younger travel partner introduces himself as Nana. They are all from Ghana. Nana says I should take "snapshots". "It's your first time in Europe, man!"

I pass him my phone and he snaps me. He says *fuck* a lot, and I wonder if the woman is his mother and where the African is in him. Nana has worked in Dubai for a few years and is in Germany on a six-month jobseeker visa, hoping to secure a work permit without having to go back to Ghana.

"This is the real deal," he says. "Africa is fucking bad. There is money in this place ehn! You can make a lot of money that you cannot even spend. But you must be really smart ehn. The best in writing in the whole of Nigeria. The whole of Nigeria! You must be really smart. And you are a pharmacist. Ah. Very lucky. If you find work here you will be rich. Fucking rich!"

Before they get to their stop, Nana and I exchange WhatsApp contacts. He says Sylt will be the last stop, so I shouldn't have any problems finding my way; he warns me though that my destination is really far. He has never been there, it is a rich white-people place. If I need any used phones or gadgets, I should let him know; I should get ready for the cold, and prepare for whiteness.

The ride across the northern part of Germany is a view of windmills and ranches, and lots of train stops and crossings. There is another train moving parallel to us on another track. It is loaded with cars moving down the track. At first I think it's a car manufacturing plant on a rail, but then I see drivers and passengers comfortably seated inside the cars atop the train.

They are moving to Sylt too, on a shuttle, crossing to the island in the comfort of their luxury cars.

iv.

Rantum is a village on the island of Sylt. I will be living in an apartment there. It is a cold, windy and flat place sandwiched between sand dunes and beaches facing the North Sea. The island is sandy and moody.

There seems to be more bicycles than humans in Sylt. Soon, I am also riding on the cycling paths of Northern Germany, nonchalantly enjoying the last of the sunny days before winter. Cycling on the island is a journey of discovery. Hitherto unknown ranches. Farmlands. Hidden paths. A seaside resort and a bourgeoisie marketplace.

But cycling is also a means to survive the winter. White people in these villages give me nods and warm smiles. These are not the surly white faces in transit at Frankfurt and Hamburg.

I learn to survive winter by cycling around the island until my legs, thighs ache, and the bones in the crack of my butt become sore. As I cycle along carefully designated bicycle paths, a bus drives past me flashing its schedule and stops on a display screen:

Linie 2

Westerland – Rantum - Hornum

The same route by bus would have cost me less than two euros; now I am ruing my decision to cycle on a ten-euro-per-day rented bicycle.

When I turned fifteen, my father surprised me with a gift: a bicycle. He drove me to the bicycle shop and I got my brand new bicycle assembled. He then drove off to work, leaving me to ride the bicycle back home. The gift was an unpleasant surprise; I was a young adult, already over the thrill of riding bicycles, at an age when learning to drive a car was what my mates did. Also, the ride home was about thirty minutes under the forty degrees heat of Sokoto. I rode the bicycle for just five minutes, my hands unsteady and wobbling, on a road without a designated cycling path, with cars honking and threatening to knock me off the road. I decided to get off the bike and walk the rest of the way home over the next hour, wheeling the bicycle along at a safe distance from the highway.

I have not ridden a bicycle again since that day.

But now, I have frequented the cycling paths of Sylt over the past few days and every ride is like a learning course in which I update my knowledge of the roads and pedestrian crossings. Every day my hands become steadier, and soon I master again the art of cycling.

I learn to survive the winter by riding rented bicycles and sweating profusely, squatting, panting. I survive the winter by walking and discovering new paths. Beaches hidden behind high-rise hotels, with a view of the North Sea. McDonald's and Burger King in a street war. Bourgeoisie streets and world-class boutiques stocking Tommy Hilfiger, Calvin Klein, and Hugo Boss. All on the same lane. All on the same street.

I survive the winter by taking a bus ride home, taking walks across dark alleys, and laughing and shouting between sand dunes and howling sea winds.

v.

I write these words on a windy night, with the speed of a racing car. It is raining; the sky is gloomy, dense and blue. The weather here translates to my own mood. Outside my apartment are empty playgrounds that would cater for the hundreds of thousands of tourist influx into Sylt in the summer. I am writing and watching all of these from my glass-enclosed porch, watching dewdrops slide down the misty glass in tiny streams. Everything outside is blurry. On my table is Toni Morrison's *Beloved*, about black bodies, black baby ghosts and haunted apartments where objects fly. The wind continues to howl, and outside, objects fly. But here in this apartment, I am a black body, prepared for whiteness.

Impossible n'est pas Camerounais[2]

Nkiacha Atemnkeng

---

[2] Originally published in *Limbe to Lagos: Nonfiction from Cameroon and Nigeria* (Lagos: Goethe-Institut Nigeria, 2018), ISBN: 978-978-968-938-5.

Impossible n'est pas Camerounais (November 1, 1971)

The white Boeing 737-200 plane with red stripes and green markings taxied on the runway and took off, ascending obliquely into the clouds. Its attention-seeking sound made the children of Douala rush out of their homes to catch a glimpse. Adults also appeared on the streets of Douala, eyes glued to the skies, pointing with quivering fingers. Airport personnel, government officials, guests and journalists at the *Aeroport International de Douala* watched the plane anxiously. Everybody basked in the marvel of Cameroon Airlines' maiden flight. The plane roared over their heads, as it made its way to Yaoundé for the first time.

"The whole of Cameroon flew into the sky that day," the grey-haired Swissport supervisor of the Douala International Airport, Jareth Michel Aimé fondly remembers the incident from a lost African magazine he had read, as he stood at the Documents Check control point, (Docs check two) in front of Gate A-22, after verifying all the passenger visas and travel documents on a South African Airways flight.

Happy chants of "Cameroun, *obosso*! Cameroun, *obosso*!" filled the air. Children sang songs reserved for airplane sightings. Adults waved at it, prayed for a safe landing. Many wished they had boarded the plane. In different Cameroonian towns, people listened to radio commentary from journalists stationed at the Douala and Yaoundé airports. The plane had disappeared from view in Douala.

The white French captain welcomed the sixty passengers on board Cameroon Airlines. He announced his co-pilot, a certain François Angounou, Cameroon's first co-pilot and captain in the making. Cameroonians on board were full of national pride. In their minds, the countdown to when co-captain Angounou will hold the reins of that Camair aircraft as main captain had begun. When the plane reached cruising altitude, six ladies dressed in colourful Camair flight attendant uniforms served sandwich, soft drinks and beer. The passengers ate and drank, listening to the soothing Makossa tunes of Manu Dibango and Francis Bebey.

Moments later, the captain announced descent into Yaoundé. The plane dipped slowly, executing its balancing trajectories towards the *Aeroport de Yaoundé*. As it landed, it was greeted by the deafening applause of a small crowd. Bare chested dancers gyrated to traditional music played with drums. Journalists reported the historic moment. They said President Ahmadou Ahidjo beamed with pride. The strength of his political will translated to the success of the first Camair flight.

The passengers disembarked from the plane to meet their associates in the arrival hall. The flight crew emerged last and made their way past the presidential guards towards the Head of State. Ahidjo was adorned in immaculate white Agbada raiment, his trademark. He stood next to the ramp, waiting for the crew with key members of his government. The crowd cheered the entire flight staff, especially François Angounou who stole the limelight from the French captain. He was the star of the day. Ahidjo shook hands with all of them. His greeting of co-pilot Angounou was special. Jareth recalls that Ahidjo complimented him in a rare tone of admiration,

"*Mon commandant!*"

The crowd cheered. The smiling Angounou stood awkwardly in front of Ahidjo, perhaps uncertain how to react to such praise from an autocratic president. Angounou completed his training later, under the patronage of Ahidjo and achieved the flight time required for full captainship. He regularly flew one of the two Boeing 737-200 planes Camair started operations with. Ahidjo made sure he wasn't poached by any other airline. Angounou naturally became Cameroon's first aviation hero, paving the way for many others to follow. He reminisced about his professional experience with Camair many years later, during an interview broadcast on national television. Ahidjo would also be the hero (not the victor) in his aviation war against Air Afrique, or precisely, against President Felix Houphouet Boigny of Cote d'Ivoire. That aviation war birthed Camair.

The Air Afrique website states that the airline was created at a conference held in Yaoundé in 1961. The idea had been discussed at two past conferences in Abidjan and Brazzaville. It was established as the official Pan-African carrier for eleven West and Central Francophone African countries--Benin, Burkina Faso, Cameroon, Central African Republic, Chad, Ivory Coast, Gabon, Mauritania, Niger, the Republic of Congo and Senegal--since they could neither launch nor maintain national carriers individually.

Air Afrique functioned smoothly throughout the Sixties, building a reputation as the most reputable carrier in West and Central Africa. However, ego problems crept in between the two *big members* in the late sixties. Air Afrique's capital had been in Abidjan. Ahidjo wanted it to be in Douala. Douala was the city with the highest traffic among the points served by the carrier in Africa at the time; Ahidjo believed that the capital should be located there. Plus, he was dissatisfied with the lack of Cameroonians in top managerial positions.

The two presidents ruffled their feathers but never came to an agreement. Ahidjo founded Cameroon Airlines on July 26th 1971. He pulled Cameroon out of the consortium in September 1971--he had been the first president in the conglomerate to do so. On November 1st, he launched Cameroon Airlines' first flight from Douala to Yaoundé. Boigny didn't have plans of pulling his country out of Air Afrique or starting a national airline. He had conceived the idea of Air Afrique at the first conference in Abidjan. So he stuck with them. Ahidjo also stuck with his Camair plan. The doomsayers at Air Afrique predicted Camair's demise. They said Ahidjo would never pull it off. But Ahidjo did on November 1st 1971. He would also show for the rest of that decade that *impossible n'est pas Camerounais*.

Sky is the Limit (1971-1981)

Ahidjo knew that for Camair to dominate the African sky like Air Afrique, he had to act fast and spend big. With Angounou on board, he proceeded to nurturing other fine Cameroonian pilots and bought good, reliable airplanes which they flew. The Camair website highlights its first fleet —two Boeing 737-200 planes and two Douglas DC-4 aircrafts--for short haul flights, as well as one Boeing 707-300 plane for long haul flights to Europe.

Construction work on the new *Aeroport International de Douala* started in the early seventies. Ahidjo inaugurated it on June 27th 1977, together with his Minister of Transport, Dr John Nkengong Monie. The new airport looked like it was going to take off itself. It was among the top five airports in sub Saharan Africa in 1977. Due to its strategic position in the middle of the gulf of Guinea, it served as the main hub of Camair. Ahidjo still wanted it to be the hub of the Central and West African states, since the old one was the dominant airport in the Air Afrique days. The Garoua International Airport in northern Cameroon was built next. It had the infrastructural capacity of serving as the hub for all the countries close to northern Africa.

Camair was the only airline landing at fourteen Cameroonian domestic airports in almost every province of the country. The airline flew to African cities such as Cotonou, Bangui, N'djamena, Brazzaville, Libreville, Malabo, Abidjan, Lagos and Dakar. It also spread tentacles globally to Paris, Marseille, Rome and Geneva. Camair recruited pilots, engineers, technicians, flight attendants and ground service staff based on merit. The Cameroonian engineers and technicians did most of their repair work at the old Douala Airport, which is near the new one.

The flight attendants radiated grace and elegance, serving with an ever-present smile. They were the embodiment of the airline's slogan, *to serve you better.* Many Camair passengers still have smitten memories of the beautiful flight attendant named Agathe Irene Ngniman. She could soothe a raging passenger during a flight with her kindness, charm and warmth. Also, Makossa artist, Ekambi Brillant plucked inspiration from the success of the airline, with a wonderful release aptly titled, "Cameroon Airlines."

Camair was a managerial success and one of the few African airlines that dominated the African sky throughout the Seventies. The company flourished with its global destinations too, especially at Charles de Gaulle in France, its busiest destination which yielded the most profits. It was a source of national pride among Cameroonian migrants there. They could eat Cameroonian food on board Camair. They could drink Cameroonian beer on board Camair. They could watch cinema on panoramic screens in English and French. And they could listen to stereo music, including the latest Makossa hits. They could also catch up with what was going on in Cameroon in French, English, Pidgin English, Duala, Ewondo, Nweh, Hausa, Baganté, or Bafut conversations. The flights were punctual. The frequencies were consistent. Flight cancellations were rare. Passengers received their luggage at arrival. And everybody looked forward to their next flight. Camair finally caught up with Air Afrique. They were both the zeitgeist. The sky was the limit for the two airlines from Francophone sub-Saharan Africa.

Cameroon is famous for her achievements in football. Camair also played a key role in the success of Cameroonian football clubs and her national team, the Indomitable Lions. The Eighties marked the first golden age of Cameroonian football and a blossoming relationship with Camair. Douala Airport trouper, Isaac Kotte still has vivid memories of the 1981 rivalry between A.S Bilima of Zaire and Canon de Yaoundé. Both teams had qualified for the two-legged final of the African Champions league. The first leg was played at the Ahmadou Ahidjo stadium in Yaoundé. A.S Bilima defeated Canon 1-0. Interestingly, Canon whitewashed A.S Bilima 3-0 at the second leg in Zaire. They absolutely stunned the Bilima fans and lifted the coveted trophy for the first time. It was the first display of Cameroonian football *hemle*.

The Bilima supporters were furious. They accused Canon of football juju, swearing in Lingala, "*Bana ba Cameroun ba zalaki sorciers!*" Sensing danger, journalist Abel Mbengue announced on radio, during his post-match report that if President Ahidjo was listening, he should try to get the Canon team out of Zaire as soon as possible. Ahidjo chartered a Camair plane to Kinshasa, which flew the victorious team back home and the whole of Yaoundé celebrated.

Combi: The eleventh province (1981)

The biggest plane Camair operated in the eighties was the Boeing 747-200, which the aircraft manufacturer, Boeing *baptised* combi—combined cargo approach. The popularity of the combi grew during the sixties. The versatile plane could be used to carry either passengers, as an airliner, or cargo as a freighter. Coincidentally, combi means "comrade" in Cameroonian Pidgin English. The plane's name also depicted its friendly relationship with the Cameroonian people. Retired state journalist, John Ndahne had been on holiday in Paris with his children, when he learnt about combi's purchase, by president Ahidjo. He had quickly secured flight tickets for his three children, who had to fly back home.

One of his sons, Nsima Ndahne, a Swissport employee himself, vividly remembers his flight experience on one of the first Paris-Douala combi trips, captained by Angounou, as he stood on the ramp writing down the pushback and take off times of an Asky Airlines plane. The ambience on board combi had been infectious. He had feasted on a meal of boiled potatoes and pepper soup. The Makossa melodies of Charles Lembe, Toto Guillaume, Nkoti François and Pierre de Moussy filtered into the aisle. The sultry voice of Anne Marie Nzie and the showy bass guitar sounds of Les Têtes Brulées boomed too. However, Ekambi Brillant's hit song, "Cameroon Airlines", eclipsed them all.

As the chatty passengers downed Cameroonian beer, the plane made its entrée into the gulf of Guinea, unveiling scenic views of the creeks and green marshlands of the Douala coast. Another classic song began thumping the plane. The shakers had sounded first. But Manu Dibango had bullied its sound away quickly, with the most vocal and most powerful of the woodwinds, deftly soloing intricate sax notes on the jazzy beat. The melody of the raucous notes alternated swiftly. Like Muhammed Ali floating on his toes before a shuffle, giving the track a very groovy tune. Manu knew how to sing with his saxophone. He finally bellowed on the song in his hoarse voice,

Hoo-haa!... Makossa brutalement civilisé.

The female back-up singers had already taken over with angelic singing in the Duala language, until they got to the song's hook,

Bienvenue, welcome to Cameroon, ouh, ouh, ouh

Bienvenue, welcome to Cameroon, ouh, ouh, ouh

Nsima Ndahne had developed goose bumps. The tipsy passengers had "ooohed" and "whoooed", marvelling at the creative musical touch to the landing concept. Combi had felt so homely even before passengers reached home. That is why Cameroonians bestowed on it an apt alias—the eleventh province. If the country had ten provinces, then combi was the eleventh. Other Cameroonians simply nicknamed combi, Mount Cameroon—the tallest mountain in West and Central Africa.

La vache à lait (1990-2000)

Douala Airport old-timer, Isaac Kotte's recollections on a sunny afternoon in the Swissport airport office that, things started to fall apart at Cameroon Airlines when Ahidjo resigned from power in 1982 are poignant. The new government wasn't as visionary with Camair as the old government had been. They had not been belligerents in the aviation war against Air Afrique. The desire to maintain the company on cloud nine just wasn't there.

Eight years after Ahidjo's resignation and death, Camair became *la vache à lait* —a cow that everybody wanted to obtain free milk from. Government officials travelled constantly on the airline on unofficial trips, with their entire families. Sometimes they even did so with their mistresses, without paying for tickets. Other passengers with Camair connections paid little to travel. Powerful companies obtained flight tickets on credit and flew their workers abroad. Camair only billed them. In most cases, the debts were paid months later or paid in half. There was a lot of laxity and little corporate governance at the airline. A dysfunctional system of checks and balances was now in place, unlike the days of Ahidjo.

Nepotism and corruption without impunity became rampant at Camair –vices which merely seeped in from a corrupt regime. *Karaa* –a word that signifies airport corruption in Cameroon became part of everyday parlance within the Douala and Nsimalen Airports. The airline was compelled to scale down operations on many destinations. The devaluation of the Franc CFA, (Cameroon's currency) and a stifling economic recession, (the country's worst since independence) further complicated matters at Camair. There was no capital which the government could inject into the airline as an economic stimulus measure.

There was no austerity measure. The airline quickly became suicidal. Like a healthy man who was putting a rope around his neck to hang himself.

The healthy cow wasn't fed enough hay to replenish its fast depleting milk reserves. It became weak and even ill. Cameroonians cried foul and lost faith in the airline, condemning the chronic mismanagement. But the cow continued to be milked excessively. Incompetent recruitments were being done based on connections, not merit anymore. Technicians and engineers were mostly employed from abroad. Camair totally regressed from what Ahidjo had envisaged; unbearable flight delays, frequent flight cancellations, stranded passengers at airports abroad, missing luggage, growing debts, overstaffing, incompetency, unpaid workers' salaries, fishy *karaa* organised by even flight crew members to obtain fast cash and keep up with their lavished life styles.

On the footballing side, the Indomitable Lions had qualified for the 1994 World Cup once again. But there was no money to send the team off to USA, as a result of the aforementioned crises. Senior researcher, Dominique Malaquais flashes back to those moments in an article published on Chimurenga Magazine. In a shocking twist of events, it was a public free will donation by Cameroonians and the country's most notorious *feyman*, Donatien Koagné, famed for being Cameroon's Robin Hood that salvaged the Indomitable Lions. Donatien appeared on state television and announced his donation of ten million Francs CFA to the team. The Indomitable Lions flew to USA where they flopped at that World Cup, even losing 6-1 to Russia. Throughout the nineties, they remained a shadow of themselves, plagued by all sorts of problems, just like their national airline and just like their country.

Founding editor of Chimurenga Magazine, Ntone Edjabe recounted his experience travelling with the Indomitable Lions during those difficult times, in a brilliant article published by the Financial Times. He narrated a story about his delayed Camair flight to South Africa. The Indomitable Lions walked on board, headed for the 1996 Africa Cup of Nations. François Oman-Biyik, scorer of the opening goal of the 1990 World Cup against Argentina and captain of the national team, didn't have a seat. One player even perched on a flight attendant's seat. The plane made an impromptu stop in Yaoundé, so the players could collect advanced payment of their match fees. After refuelling stops in Kinshasa and Harare, the plane arrived in Johannesburg eight hours late. The Indomitable Lions moved directly to the stadium, where South Africa's Bafana Bafana was waiting. And Cameroon was walloped 3-0. Gone were the days when special Camair planes were chartered to fly home victorious football clubs and the indomitable national team from World Cups. They now had to gate crash overloaded and delayed commercial Camair flights.

Sortie de piste (2000-2008)

The Camair website reveals that, two Camair planes were involved in minor accidents in the late eighties, leading to one or two casualties. However, it was on December 3rd 1995 that the angel of death fully visited the airline. The beleaguered company experienced its worst accident in history. Flight 3701, which was operated by a Boeing 737-200 plane, experienced a problem with its landing gear and crashed near Douala, killing 71 out of the 76 passengers on board. Camair's already battered reputation was completely ruined.

In November 2000, flight 70, operated by good, old combi flew from Douala to Paris. As it attempted landing, it veered off the runway at the Charles de Gaulle Airport, causing the front landing gear to be torn off and the legendary plane being damaged beyond repair. All the passengers on board were evacuated alive, including the minister delegate at the ministry of Finance, Roger Tchoungui and Cameroonian music star, Beko Sadey. It was an accident which the press named *sortie de piste*. Though there weren't any casualties in that mishap, it was the physical sign that Camair the sick cow had finally fainted and gone into a coma. The airline made its sortie out of the African aviation market for good.

Clients fled to other airlines with fast growing reputations. Not Air Afrique though. The pan-African airline was also being plagued by similar managerial problems. Air Afrique went defunct in 2002 but Camair remained in its comma, occasionally operating flights until 2008. Emerging players had however come into the game, filling the void Camair and Air Afrique created. Kenya Airways (which was launched six years after Camair in 1977), was now the big boy of the sub Saharan African sky. Their slogan, *the pride of Africa*, was fitting. They paraded their white planes with red and green stripes and their K-tails like Kangaroos; stepping, taxiing, hopping and taking giant leaps into space in Neil Armstrong boastfulness.

On 16th September 2005, the French Civil Aviation Authority banned Camair from operating its prestigious Paris route. It was due to safety concerns that had arisen following aircraft check-ups that revealed failures to meet international norms. That was the final straw that broke the cow's back. A desperate effort to save Cameroon Airlines from bankruptcy through an agreement with SN Airholding failed. Instead, the launch of Cameroon Airlines Corporation, Camair-Co, as the new national airline was announced in 2006, following a presidential decree by Paul Biya. Camair finally ceased all its operations and self-destructed in March 2008.

The Phoenix (2011-2017)

Camair-Co launched flight operations in 2011. The inaugural flight from Douala to Yaoundé and then Paris, took place on March 28th. The airline started with a fleet of three planes, six domestic routes and nine international destinations. Ethiopian Airlines' engineers and technicians were contracted to do Camair-Co's maintenance work. The airline has been making losses since its creation, according to many local newspapers and Wikipedia, prompting government stimulus measures. The state has also been changing its General Directors almost annually, to ameliorate the ever-growing problems afflicting the young airline. There have been five of them on the hot seat after only six years. The old phoenix is slowly rising from the ashes.

A former Camair employee, Eyango Samuel, who now works for Swissport as a *profiler*, stood at his Documents Check post in the check-in hall (Docs check one), after rounding off work on an Ethiopian Airlines flight. Camair-Co's check-in was in full swing. A conversation with a few of his colleagues about what transpires at Camair-Co sprang up, as they all dismantled the Ethiopian Airlines counter poles. And Eyango revealed some very disconcerting information. He said the inner core of the new airline still comprises of the same *autochthones* who were at the helm at Camair. They work for their own interests, not the betterment of the airline. They prey on younger, more ambitious and more competent colleagues.

Private media in Cameroon reported that an attempt was made to burn some of the Camair-Co offices in Yaoundé in 2015, by many disgruntled passengers. They all complained of the same poor services that hampered Camair in the nineties. Camair-Co ceased operations on its Paris route not long after launch –its only European destination, due to a "restructuring policy". However, Rwandair which started operations under that name in 2009 has rapidly increased its fleet to twelve planes. Camair-Co's fleet still consists of five planes. Rwandair now flies to twenty-two cities, including intercontinental flights to Dubai, Mumbai, London and Brussels.

In 2014, it was TAAG Angola, a small unknown Angolan airline that flew the Indomitable Lions to the World Cup in Brazil. Not Camair-Co. They lost all their three games in the first round and were bundled out of the competition early. Even though Camair-Co flew them back to Yaoundé from Libreville as 2017 African champions for the fifth time, the suicide of Camair and its troubled phoenix rising from the ashes, still hurts many Cameroonians, especially those of the seventies generation who basked in its glorious sunshine.

Vert le passeport, amers les aéroports

Anne Marie Befoune

Je ne suis pas de ceux qui pensent qu'on devrait faire de l'Afrique un grand pays. Les frontières de chaque territoire ont leur importance et ne devraient être abolies. Chaque pays africain doit se développer indépendamment des autres en se focalisant sur ses singularités, sur la manière d'en faire un levier de développement social puis économique. Une fois le mécanisme mis en place et les fruits récoltés, des collaborations pérennes et sur un pied d'égalité devraient être établies pour un Continent fort.

Je suis de ceux qui croient en l'importance des frontières, mais je suis également de ceux qui en souffrent. Il m'est aujourd'hui quasiment impossible d'accéder à certains pays, quelle que soit la raison pour laquelle je souhaite m'y rendre. Peu de pays que j'ai la possibilité de visiter m'accueillent à bras ouverts ou à cachet facile… Je ne suis pas de ceux qui peuvent voyager sur un coup de tête à travers le continent. Je n'ose parler d'au-delà.

Je suis Camerounaise.

Ainsi dit, cela semble anodin. Il existe des millions de Camerounais à travers le monde, alors ce n'est pas une réelle particularité. Jusqu'à ce qu'on décide de voyager ou jusqu'à ce qu'on s'adonne à des occupations qui requièrent de fréquents déplacements. C'est mon cas depuis quelques années. Si je devais raconter mes déboires à travers les ambassades et aéroports à travers le monde, je ne saurais par où commencer.

Mon voyage loupé au Zimbabwé parce qu'il me fallait un visa au contraire de mes collègues, et qu'aucune des représentations présente dans le pays où je vis n'en délivrait? Ou encore mon visa de 4 jours pour Paris alors que ceux avec qui je m'y rendais se sont vus accorder des accès multiples pour un minimum de 6 mois et un maximum de deux ans? Mon passeport retenu à la descente d'avion au Botswana et au Burkina Faso? Ou mieux, mon passeport à peine regardé au consulat du Maroc alors que je remplissais toutes les conditions d'éligibilité et que j'avais en ma possession une invitation en bonne et due forme de l'Union Africaine?

Chaque voyage annoncé est pour moi cause de stress. Je suis généralement la seule Camerounaise du groupe, donc, la seule pour qui il faut se démener, la seule susceptible de ne pas partir. C'est toujours les yeux écarquillés que ma réponse « J'ai besoin d'un visa pour y aller » est reçue. Très peu de pays m'accordent une entrée sans visa, ou encore un visa à l'arrivée. Malgré son prix coûteux, mon passeport n'a pas grande importance pour les autres. Au contraire, il est source de suspicion.

J'ai l'impression d'être jugée chaque fois que quelqu'un tient mon passeport entre ses mains. Lorsque je dois sortir du Sénégal, pays dans lequel je vis depuis quelques années déjà, je m'habille le plus simplement possible, et m'assure de disposer par-devers moi d'une copie imprimée de chacun des papiers utiles à ma demande de visa ou qui pourrait prouver la raison pour laquelle je sors du territoire. Mon cœur a manqué un battement lorsqu'un agent de la police des frontières m'a fait remarquer une fois que je voyageais « beaucoup », et parfois pour des pays « très éloignés ». Étais-je soupçonnée d'un trafic quelconque ? Avais-je l'air d'une criminelle ?

Je ne mets pas d'épingles dans les cheveux. Je ne porte pas de ceinture. Je ne porte pas de chaussettes. Je ne laisse aucune chance au détecteur à métaux de sonner lorsque je le traverse. Je m'assure que le livre que je lis ne peut être considéré comme subversif. Je ne parle pas. Je m'arrange à voyager seule autant que possible. Et, surtout, je ne brandis pas mon passeport sous tous les nez. Il est retourné lorsqu'il est visible, alors, il est impossible d'y lire « République du Cameroun ». Je ne me déplace pas à l'intérieur des pays dans lesquels je réside. Je ne fais pas de tourisme. Je me limite à ma chambre d'hôtel et la salle de conférences. Je me fais discrète pour ne pas être interpellée. Comment expliquer que je suis une Camerounaise qui déambule dans les rues?

Tout ceci peut sembler excessif, mais ne l'est pas. Il faut l'avouer, être Camerounais n'est pas une bénédiction lorsqu'on voyage beaucoup. Pourtant, malgré l'accueil froid et les doutes récurrents en rapport avec chacune des informations contenues dans mon passeport, je ne me plains pas du traitement qui est mien. Je n'en veux pas aux personnes en face de moi. Je ne leur en veux pas de me réduire à ma nationalité. Tout ceci est bien pénible, mais s'explique aisément.

Les Camerounais n'ont pas bonne presse hors des frontières de leur pays. Ils n'ont pas bonne presse dans leur propre pays s'il faut être honnête. Chaque époque a eu sa vague. Les années quatre-vingt et quatre-vingt-dix ont été la période de gloire de ceux qui se faisaient appeler des Feymen, et dont Donatien Koagne a été le porte-étendard. Ces hommes se rendaient dans les pays les plus éloignés et se faisaient passer pour des rois, des ministres ou encore des êtres doués de pouvoirs surnaturels qui leur permettaient de multiplier les billets de banque. Des arnaques sans précédent en ont résulté.

Les années 2000 ont été celles de l'accès à internet, et donc d'arnaques plus sophistiquées. Des personnes en mal d'amour à travers le monde ont vidé leur compte en banque pour assister une bien-aimée fictive vue dont la situation familiale allait toujours de mal en pis. Des princes africains devant faire sortir leur fortune de leur pays ont eu accès à des comptes en banque de personnes naïves, comptes en banque vidés sans aucun scrupule. Des milliers d'hectares de terrains boisés inexistants ont été vendus à des millions d'euros à travers le Cameroun. Des jeunes dames qui avaient réussi à mettre le grappin sur des blancs faisaient « monter » leurs sœurs avec les papiers français reçus quelque temps après leur mariage.

Les années 2010 ont été marquées par l'immigration clandestine, mais aussi des moyens de survie dangereux pour les ressortissants des pays d'accueil: drogue, prostitution, arnaques, braquages…

Je ne suis rien d'autre qu'une victime des méfaits de mes compatriotes, tout comme ceux qui en ont directement souffert, c'est-à-dire ceux-là qui me regardent avec suspicion et hésitent à m'ouvrir les portes de leur pays malgré mon casier judiciaire vierge et la preuve de l'activité qui m'y emmène. Je ne peux leur en vouloir de me demander avec agressivité quand est-ce que je partirai de chez eux, ce que je fais toujours immédiatement l'activité terminée.

Je ne peux en vouloir aux ambassades de vouloir protéger leur pays d'autres Camerounais, de ces gens qui leur rappellent certainement des souvenirs qu'ils auraient préféré oublier. Je ne peux en vouloir aux policiers des frontières lorsqu'ils froncent le nez et me demandent si l'âge sur mon passeport est vraiment le mien. Beaucoup de jeunes filles ont voyagé avec les papiers de leur grande ou leur petite sœur, et beaucoup de faux passeports originaires du Cameroun ont circulé. Je ne suis peut-être pas une faussaire, mais je porte la marque laissée par toutes ces personnes venant de chez moi, la marque de chacun de leurs méfaits.

Je n'en veux certes à personne, mais je suis lassée. Je suis lassée de devoir planifier chaque voyage des mois à l'avance. Je suis lassée de ne pas planifier de vacances parce que ma demande de visa ne sera accompagnée d'aucune lettre d'une organisation respectée qui, à défaut de témoigner de mon honnêteté, se porte garante de mes va-et-vient. Je suis lassée d'être toujours de la catégorie des « sauf ». Vous ne la connaissez pas? Alors vous ne connaissez certainement pas la phrase « Accessible sans visa/visa délivré à l'arrivée *sauf* pour les ressortissants des pays suivants ».

Je dois avouer avoir souvent pensé à changer de nationalité. Encore quelques années de vie au Sénégal, et je pourrai introduire mon dossier pour devenir fille de la Terranga. Les origines de ma mère me donnent également la possibilité de déchirer mon passeport vert et d'accéder à un autre d'une couleur moins traumatisante. Cette idée me traverse l'esprit chaque fois que je me rends compte qu'une fois de plus je fais partie des « sauf », chaque fois que je pense que le chemin de croix que m'imposent les ambassades aurait pu être évité. Je ne sais si je finirai par le faire. Ce que je sais en tout cas est que je ne souhaite à aucun Camerounais de passer sa nationalité à son enfant. Cet innocent se retrouvera comme moi, coupable de méfaits dont il ne sait rien.

Partir

c'est mourir un peu

Florian Ngimbis

Aller à l'étranger quand on est camerounais… Un calvaire selon certains, un conte surréaliste pour d'autres.

Les théories abondent : faux documents, multiplication de méfaits à l'étranger, escroqueries multiples via la fameuse feymania, divers types d'arnaques rendues plus faciles par l'interconnexion via le cyberespace, chacun y va de sa science pour expliquer cette méfiance quasi universelle que l'humain du vingt et unième siècle semble éprouver pour le Camerounais.

Ressenti parfois surfait, considérant la complexité pour d'autres nationalités, d'emprunter un avion pour un malheureux voyage du "bon côté" du "monde libre" post 11 septembre.

Néanmoins, dans le lexique du Camerounais du vingt et unième siècle, emprunter un moyen de transport pour aller d'un point A vers un point B à l'intérieur du pays se dit "se déplacer". Emprunter un avion pour aller d'un point A à l'intérieur du pays vers un point B à l'extérieur se dit "Voyager". La figure d'atténuation/insistance suggère que, n'a jamais vraiment voyagé que celui qui s'est lancé dans le parcours d'obstacles que constitue trop souvent l'obtention d'un visa, autorisation d'entrer dans un pays étranger, européen notamment.

ℬ

Le récital commence par la valse délirante des ambassades dont les exigences donneraient le tournis au plus aguerri des danseurs. Documents étranges, exigences ubuesques, délais lilliputiens… Tout semble mis en œuvre dans les chancelleries caucasiennes pour refréner le désir de départ. L'ensemble de la procédure nimbée d'un accueil froid et condescendant qui fait du requérant un demandeur larmoyant plus qu'un voyageur insouciant.

En ces temps malheureux, certaines chancelleries poussent le vice jusqu'à l'exigence d'un pointage à l'ambassade dans un délai explicite après le retour. Les joies de la nationalité camerounaise… Ce plaisir constant de côtoyer les tréfonds de l'inconsidération. L'exigence de décaper son enveloppe noire de pauvreté, de précarité, pour pouvoir montrer patte blanche et entrer au "paradis" blanc.

Mais la valse n'est que l'ouverture. Le voyageur camerounais qui comme moi est jeune, négligemment vêtu et surtout voyage léger, bénéficie très souvent d'un traitement particulier dans les aéroports. Un certain regard, eu égard à l'aura malfaisante qui émane de lui. Ces vibrations faites de suspicion d'émigration économique, de clandestinité future, soutenue par un quelconque trafic interlope. Trop souvent sous ces latitudes, partir c'est mourir un peu. Mourir dans le regard des autres, au départ, à l'arrivée, à l'accueil, en transit. Des autres qui jugent, supputent, flairent, interrogent, concluent. Des autres qui vous mettent dans une case, une tombe creusée par les louvoiements géopolitiques, une case dans laquelle le respect est fonction d'un passeport, dont la nationalité détermine s'il sera une oriflamme triomphante ou le linceul du mépris et du rejet.

Avril 2015
Seconde année en tant que jury monde francophone du concours international Bob's (Best of The Blogs), je suis, comme chaque année, invité à Berlin pour siéger en compagnie de personnalités du monde de l'activisme en ligne. Un grand oral qui débouche sur la désignation du vainqueur du concours.

Procédure de visa à l'ambassade d'Allemagne à Yaoundé. Même si l'accueil est moins froid que chez les homologues de l'autre rive du Rhin, je subis néanmoins le stress lié à la production d'un nombre incroyable de documents attestant d'inutilités que, quelqu'un quelque part a jugé utiles pour me laisser fouler le sol européen.

Passeport tamponné et rendu in extremis. Quelques heures plus tard, je suis en route pour emprunter un vol Air France nocturne. Je traverse avec amertume le hall du hangar pompeusement appelé aéroport. Triste, moche, dépassé, déprimant.

File pour se faire contrôler avant l'enregistrement. Quelqu'un me tapote l'épaule avec toute l'amabilité de ceux de ma nationalité.

—Mon frère, bonsoir. Je demande hein, tu prends le Air France pour Paris ?

Je ne suis pas son frère, mais ça fait longtemps que je n'ai pas ouvert la bouche. Le chauffeur de taxi, du genre taciturne n'a presque pas pipé mot durant les vingt et quelques kilomètres de mon domicile à l'aéroport.

—Peut-être.

J'aime ça, les répliques idiotes, façon série B.

—Tu as des kilos ?

—Non.

—Mais... À part ton sac à dos, je ne vois pas de valise.

C'est que je voyage léger. Moins d'une semaine à Berlin, à part des sous-vêtements et des t-shirts, je ne vois pas pourquoi m'encombrer de bagages inutiles.

Le frère insiste. Il est prêt à me refiler toute une valise, et le prix qu'il me propose est plus qu'alléchant.

—Frère, je vais en Allemagne, je transite juste par Charles de Gaulle.

Il a la solution : quelqu'un peut passer prendre le colis à Berlin. Je commence à perdre patience.

—Akié ! Mon Frère, je dis que ne peux pas prendre ton colis, je suis désolé.

Je me souviens de son regard, un mélange de points d'interrogation et de têtes de mort au milieu de questions et de sarcasmes non exprimés mais reconnaissables :

Ekié ! Tu refuses l'argent ?

C'est même un Camerounais ça ?

N'est-ce pas tu pars caler à Mbeng ?

Mouf chien vert tu crois même que quoi ?

Disparue la fausse politesse. Disparue la fraternité de circonstance. Son regard mauvais me fouaille la conscience avant que l'ex frère me tourne ostensiblement le dos.

Je présente mon passeport à l'officier effectuant le tri à l'entrée de l'aire d'enregistrement.

Surprise. Il s'agit d'une vieille connaissance. Un de ces jeunes ignares, devenu policier par la force de l'équilibre régional, passé officier par la puissance des réseaux et nommé à un poste à l'aéroport par un quelconque mystère puant du trafic d'influence.

Des lustres qu'on ne s'est pas vus.

« Euye ! Ngimbis tu vas à mbeng ? »

Question rhétorique. Je souris, jaune koki.

« Tu n'as pas de valise ? Mon frère, tu pars caler c'est ça ? »

Je souris toujours. Jaune sauce jaune.

« Mon frère, Mbeng n'est pas facile hein… Mais je t'encourage. Le pays est trop compliqué. »

À cause de connards de ton espèce oui.

Je souris en ravalant mon fiel et ma réplique. La capacité de nuisance d'un policier est l'une des dernières valeurs sûres de ce pays…

Enregistrement. La jeune employée des Aéroports du Cameroun ne sourit pas. Pas désagréable non plus. Elle fait juste son travail. Professionnellement.

« Destination ?

—Berlin

—Bagages à mettre en soute ?

—Aucun, Madame. »

Elle lève le sourcil. Je pense d'abord que c'est à cause du "Madame", parfois rare sous nos latitudes où on lui préfère "ma chérie". Puis je vois qu'elle considère mon sac à dos, mes dreads et lance un regard entendu à sa collègue et voisine de comptoir. Le regard est silencieux, mais je peux lire en filigrane une phrase : *en voilà encore un qui ne rentrera pas.*

J'avale deux gorgées de salive amère, récupère mes papiers et rejoins le hangar d'embarquement.

Paris Charles de Gaulle, plusieurs heures et un mauvais repas plus tard. Police aux Frontières.

« Papiers monsieur ! »

Dans sa niche de verre, le molosse ausculte mon passeport, le scanne, le palpe, le gratte, le renifle presque.

« Destination ?

– Berlin.

– Raison du voyage ? »

Je voudrais être à égalité avec lui : faire des réponses aussi laconiques que ses questions.

« Jury de concours.

– Pardon ?

—Je suis membre d'un jury de concours.

—Profession ? »

Je ricane intérieurement en lançant :

« Blogueur.

—Pardon ?

—Blogueur. » Il encaisse en silence.

« Vous avez une invitation ? »

Ah… ça devient amusant.

Je sors une invitation, en allemand…

—Vous ne l'avez pas en français ?

—Non Monsieur, je parle la langue. Je peux vous la traduire si vous voulez.

Rougeoiement des oreilles qu'il a grandes et écartées.

—Vous avez une assurance voyage ?

Bien sûr que oui. Tout subsaharien aux cheveux crépus sait qu'à tout moment, c'est-à-dire très souvent, en plus de ses documents de voyage, d'autres peuvent lui être exigés. Assurance, réservation d'hôtel, moyens de subsistance, lettre d'invitation etc.

Aussi le subsaharien se promène-t-il avec une chemise en carton ou en plastique non biodégradable qui renferme tous ces précieux sésames.

Mes multiples déplacements et surtout les déconvenues dans les aéroports du "monde libre" m'ont formé. Je suis prêt. Mi-moqueur, mi-arrogant, je dégaine chaque document demandé en souriant.

« Retour prévu ?

— Samedi soir.

— Ce samedi ? »

J'acquiesce en me moquant de son coup d'œil semblant me dire : tu ne me prends pas pour un con là ?

« Vous logez où à Berlin s'il vous plaît ? »

Moi, dans mon plus incompréhensible allemand : « Wallstraße 23-24, 10179 Berlin »

Je jouis presque en égrenant sans respirer zehntausend hundert neun und siebzig…

— Chez des parents ?

— Non un quatre-étoiles, très joli.

Là, le pandore comprend enfin que je me paye poliment sa tête.

Dernier regard noir. Coup de tampon réticent et mon passeport vert ndolè retrouve le confort relatif de ma poche.

« Bon voyage Monsieur. »

J'adore ce mépris à la française. Tout est dans le fond. Difficile à décrypter car enrobé dans une pilule visqueuse d'hypocrisie sucrée.

« Au revoir chef ! »

Aéroport de Berlin Tegel, quelques heures et une collation plus tard…
J'ai dormi.

Même le contrôle aléatoire dans la file du contrôle de sûreté des bagages cabine ne m'émeut pas. J'ai parié contre moi-même que si quelqu'un dans la file se faisait contrôler dans mon environnement direct, ce serait moi. Bingo. Je suis riche de mille francs et tout aussi pauvre de la même somme.

Je repense à tout cela en me dirigeant vers la sortie de l'aéroport. Je me sens moins oppressé. Je souris même en repensant au policier de Charles de Gaulle, je souris encore plus en pensant à mon sourire quand j'y repenserai sous une douche bien chaude, dans la proximité d'un lit paré de draps frais.

J'ai presque atteint la sortie…

Please sir…

Deux types qu'on dirait tout droit sortis de la série policière *Un cas pour deux* m'encadrent et me font signe de les suivre. Les sosies de Josef Matula me conduisent dans un local et m'expliquent dans un anglais à couper à la tronçonneuse qu'ils vont devoir fouiller mon sac à dos. Dans le même élan, il m'est demandé et si j'ai des choses à déclarer.

Des douaniers.

Fouille au corps minutieuse effectuée par le premier, tandis que je vois le second se jeter comme un fauve sur mon sac à dos muni d'un coton-tige. C'est là que je comprends. Ils cherchent de la drogue…

Pour la première fois mon flegme et mon impassibilité m'ont abandonné et c'est d'une voix étranglée j'ai lancé un : Ekié! C'est comment chef ?

Maroua – Kousséri:

No man's land!

Raoul Djimeli

L'enfer est une chanson! Une sorte d'incantation, lente au rythme, avec des mots en français qu'on entend seulement si le car entre et ressort brutalement d'un trou, obligeant la dame à saccader la voix. La voiture sonde le désert en creusant la poussière. Nous sommes agrippés à ses vieux sièges. Sur ma gauche, une jeune mère d'une vingtaine d'années, le visage sec, les lèvres rouges d'un maquillage trop visible, les yeux clairs. De temps en temps elle pose son fils sur mes jambes, sans demander mon avis. Elle recouvre la couche de poussière sur ses lèvres par une nouvelle couche de rouge à lèvres. Accroché à son sein, son petit garçon ne fait pas attention à l'Apocalypse. Il regarde le paysage infini à travers une vitre fendillée et suce tranquillement l'immense sein que sa mère plante dans sa bouche comme pour narguer la soif des passagers.

Décembre a sonné ses cloches! Le matin, le soleil se lève derrière les montagnes jaunes de sécheresse. Le voyage commence doucement. Sur un mince ruban de bitume, nous entamons notre montée vers la dernière ville du Cameroun. Au départ, le climat est rude, mais pas tant que ça, car, le vent est encore normal. Bientôt, le bitume disparaît, le climat se complique et doucement, le voyage se transforme en supplice. Parfois, nous passons près d'un berger malchanceux: quelqu'un qui cherchait un point d'eau et désormais statufié devant la réalité d'un lac séché. Le passage de notre voiture l'enveloppe d'un nuage de poussière d'où jaillit le bêlement assoiffé de ses moutons. Dehors, la beauté du paysage arrache la vue. Le soleil crache ses rayons violents sur les petits villages chanceux: ceux que la guerre a oubliés.

Elle chante, elle chante et lorsqu'elle renouvelle sa couche de maquillage, elle se tait. Assis sur mes jambes, son fils la regarde faire.

Maroua – Kousséri! Combien de kilomètres cela fait-il ? Il faut poser la question aux Chinois à qui jadis, le chantier fut offert. Aujourd'hui il y a le désert, la nouvelle route touristique au cœur des boko haram. Et puis il n'y a rien d'autre. Peut-être, des villages: trois, quatre, cinq ou six familles qui, incapables de fuir la terreur, attendent. Après tout, elle est partout, la mort. Elle se glisse à dos de choléra, juchée sur un palu que personne ne soigne et peut-être aussi cachée dans les rayons du soleil rouge qui mange les os des petits enfants.

—Il y aura le convoi des militaires armés pour nous protéger, me lance la jeune mère.

Je ne réponds pas. C'est une route que je connais : lorsque j'ai emprunté le désert l'an passé, je sortais du Cameroun pour la première fois. Si quelqu'un m'avait sorti les mêmes mots en cette occasion, j'aurais engagé un long exposé qui aurait certainement débouché sur la présentation de mon passeport. J'aurais fait des comparaisons en comptant sur mon passeport pour défendre mes propos. Ah ! Le passeport! La preuve qu'on fait le monde! Qu'on sait toujours de quoi on parle, qu'on a raison sur tous les sujets, qu'on mérite toujours mieux! Je me serais plaint de l'état du désert, des conditions du voyage, du froid qui fendille les lèvres.

Celui qui n'a voyagé qu'une fois est prisonnier. Il passe sa vie à embêter les autres. L'an dernier j'étais prisonnier. Depuis, j'ai visité d'autres pays. Je sais que partout, la vie est la même. Je sais qu'il y a dans le pays le mieux construit du monde, une route impossible, des gens imbéciles et un climat insupportable pour qui vient de loin. Je sais que d'où je viens, le coin de la terre où je pisse est un eldorado pour quelqu'un qui viendra. La jeune dame redit sa phrase en reposant son enfant sur moi. Je ne fais aucun commentaire.

L'an dernier, je n'ai pas eu besoin qu'on me dise qu'il y avait des militaires pour nous protéger sur le chemin. J'avais annoncé à Romuald, mon grand frère, que je sortais du pays, que je voyageais par route. Que je sortais par la zone où il *militait* avec foi. Je venais d'avoir mon passeport, j'avais même manqué un voyage pour le Maroc. Avant d'entamer la route pour le Tchad, j'avais écrit à Cilas : « Oncle, j'ai eu mon passeport, je cherche des occasions ; les sites de bourses et les appels à financement sont tellement bourrés d'infos et de détails que je ne sais plus quoi faire. Je filtre, mais je ne peux suivre aucune piste jusqu'au bout. Compliqué ! Si tu trouves quelque chose de moins compliqué, un appel qui concerne les gens de mon domaine, écris-moi, s'il te plaît ». Par la suite, je lui avais rappelé ce qu'était « mon domaine » : les langues, la littérature, les *cultural studies*, la communication et le journalisme.

Cilas ne m'a jamais répondu.

Après Mora, dans un petit village de rien du tout, j'avais croisé Romuald qu'aucun membre de la famille n'avait vu depuis qu'il avait rejoint les rangs d'Honneur et Fidélité, la Grande Muette. Romuald galérait là, sur la route des terroristes.

— Regarde, *ô djio nzem gha nor*? Tout ça c'est le Nigéria. C'est par là-bas qu'ils viennent. *Po zing te nkuo moh jih'a, mbu neng mok'u* !

— Et vous risquez vos vies comme ça chaque jour pour qu'on vous paye trente-six mille francs ?

— Petit-frère, laisse ! C'est Honneur et Fidélité !

L'année dernière, en allant à Kousseri, j'ai vu mon frère au front. Cette année-là, il y eut assez d'émotions dans l'air pour me faire oublier la route de l'enfer!

Cette année, je sens l'enfer me traverser.

La jeune mère veut déposer son fils sur mes jambes mais l'enfant refuse de lâcher le sein. Il s'y accroche avec application. La mère sourit, elle me regarde. Ses lèvres sont maintenant blanches de poussière. Je fais semblant de ne pas regarder le spectacle. Avec le pouce et l'index, j'essaye de nettoyer mes yeux, d'apprécier le tableau que le désert offre aux voyageurs tétanisés et nerveux.

J'essaye de raconter le voyage à Likress chez qui j'ai passé la nuit, mon téléphone me signale qu'il n'y a pas de couverture réseau. Mais je constate que j'ai reçu des messages une heure plus tôt. C'est elle qui voulait s'enquérir du voyage. Elle m'a raconté tôt le matin, avant que je ne parte, que certains cars qui quittent Maroua n'arrivent jamais à destination. Que parfois, on n'en retrouve aucune trace. Elle s'est inquiétée, mais je l'ai rassurée sans vraiment savoir si j'arriverais à destination. Cela fait deux ans qu'elle vit à Maroua. Nous avons passé le concours d'entrée à l'École Normale de Maroua ensemble. Elle, admise. Moi, recalé. Je ne l'avais pas revue depuis. J'ai eu beaucoup de bonheur à la revoir. Hier, à Maroua, elle m'a accueilli dans sa petite chambre d'étudiante. Elle m'a présenté au garçon qu'elle fréquente... Un certain Aimé, ingénieur. Je suis reparti à 4 heures. Elle m'a accompagné à la gare et a attendu que le car démarre. Il était 6 heures.

Autour de 10 heures, nous arrivons finalement dans le petit village où le convoi de militaires nous attend. C'est un petit marché très animé. Un homme y joue même de la musique. Assis à l'ombre, les passagers attendent que le convoi des militaires donne le signal aux chauffeurs de démarrer. Je vois la jeune mère se diriger derrière un buisson d'herbes sèches, je l'observe s'accroupir et se relever. Son fils est attaché dans le dos. Comme elle, beaucoup de personnes se soulagent dans l'immensité du vide.

Elle avance vers les vendeurs réunis sous les branches, achète du poulet frit et de l'eau en sachet. Je termine mon plat de couscous en avalant le dernier morceau de viande.

Cette année, mon frère n'est plus en route. Il a été affecté dans le grand Sud.

Bientôt, les militaires font signe aux passagers d'entrer dans les voitures. Mes membres m'élancent. Je regarde notre véhicule, parqué comme des dizaines d'autres. Je pense au supplice qui va recommencer. À l'enfant que la jeune mère déposera sur mes jambes parce qu'il n'y a même pas le moindre espace pour reculer le pied, tellement les gens sont serrés. Mes jambes sont lourdes, mais il faut entrer.

Il y a une semaine, j'étais à Lagos, puis à Abéokuta, Ogun State. Avant, j'ai eu la chance de découvrir le Benin, le Togo, le Ghana et le Maroc. Chaque fois, c'était le luxe. J'étais invité par des grandes organisations qui s'occupaient de moi comme la jeune mère de son fils. Chaque fois c'était le luxe. Me voici sur la route des boko haram, pour une fois de plus rallier N'Djaména, où on me connaît déjà. Je viens encore pour un festival, mais je ne suis plus vraiment invité. Je traverse la route de l'enfer, avec mon propre argent. L'excitation est partie depuis Yaoundé, quand j'ai payé le ticket pour mes deux premiers jours de voyage. Nous roulons à une vitesse inacceptable. Parfois, les roues du car décollent du sol et les passagers crient. Nous sommes toujours surpris de ne pas faire de tonneau. Le désert s'écarte comme la gueule d'un loup. Nous y roulons. Paul Biya ne considère peut-être plus cette partie du Cameroun comme partie intégrante du triangle national. Aucune infrastructure, rien qui signale la présence d'un État.

Nous fendons le désert dans une vieille voiture rouillée. Je suis assis juste à côté de la portière, c'est une aubaine. J'ai le pied droit qui peut aller un peu plus loin, au niveau de cette portière, le pied gauche est hélas condamné à l'immobilité. C'est là que la jeune mère installe son fils. Je sens mon genou me détester, je sens ma force me quitter.

Il y a eu des contrôles de police au début du chemin, chaque arrêt devenant une occasion de réconciliation entre mon pied gauche et moi-même. Les seuls moments du voyage durant lesquels mon corps reconquiert un semblant d'humanité. Maintenant il n'y a plus de contrôles. Nous suivons seulement les mitraillettes des militaires qui nous montrent le chemin. Tout le long, nous sommes des ombres blanches qui oscillent et s'envolent dans le vaste désert.

Combien de temps avant l'arrivée? Personne ne répond. Peu de gens parlent français. Dans le bus du désert, il y a un jeune qui chante maintenant du gospel nigérian. On dirait qu'il sent la mort venir. Il chante que rien n'est perdu. Qu'il faut garder la foi. Que s'il marche dans la vallée de l'ombre de la mort, il ne craint rien. Lorsque le véhicule du désert plonge dans un trou gigantesque, j'entends:

— *Chinéké mé* !

La roue est déchirée. Impossible d'avancer. L'homme de Dieu cesse de chanter. Les autres véhicules nous dépassent en pleurant notre sort. Le dernier véhicule de militaires passe près de nous comme s'il n'avait pas remarqué notre présence. Autour de nous, la mort sent. On ne voit rien, mais on sait que les boko haram ne sont pas loin. Que leur prière est de voir ce genre de choses arriver. L'enfant pleure. Le chauffeur nous fait signe de descendre. Aidé par quelques personnes, il change rapidement la roue. Quelques minutes plus tard, nous voilà repartis.

Le désert s'étend à perte de vue. La route n'existe pas. Il faut foncer dans ce néant. Les camions viennent dans tous les sens, chargés comme au dernier jour. Je les regarde passer près de moi, ou là-bas, au loin. Le désert continue. Il est infini! J'essaye de dormir sur mes os fatigués. Quelques instants après, je me réveille avec l'envie irrépressible de marcher un peu. Aucune chance! Nous avons rejoint le bras le plus sombre de ce désert: le fief même de boko haram. On peut voir les carcasses des voitures brûlées, juste là, dans l'herbe jaunie par la misère. Les militaires nous ont devancés. Ils roulent à tombeau ouvert dans des pick-up de guerre, une mitrailleuse devant le nez de quiconque essaie une attaque. Ils vont à la vitesse de l'éclair, et mille voitures les suivent. Il faut rester concentré, me dis-je. Peut-être qu'il y a une chance d'échapper au désert, de prendre la route, si elle existe. Rien: le désert est une chanson qui se répète! Dans l'engin qui nous transporte, il faut danser sur cet air; rester courageux et concentré!

Il faut créer dans son imagination, quelque chose de moins difficile que la mort, il faut devenir poète. Prendre à témoin ce désert qui nous regarde et dont on aura besoin un peu, dans une histoire ou dans une autre. Il faut penser à la vie et penser au retour qui est dans une semaine. Ce n'est pas la mer à boire. Pourvu que les boko haram ne sortent pas de leur cachette. Nous roulons comme on peut, impossible de rattraper le convoi.

Le désert ne finit pas: les carcasses s'allongent toujours. Nous voyons les pick-up des militaires s'en retourner. Ils ont escorté les chanceux à l'autre bout. Ils nous font signe de nous arrêter, pour s'assurer que notre véhicule n'est pas pris en otage. Ils vérifient les cartes d'identité, puis nous font signe de circuler. Les sacs sont bien attachés sur le porte-bagages; si le caoutchouc les reliant cédait à cet instant, on aurait deux choix: mourir tous ensemble ou laisser les bagages aux seigneurs du désert. Le désert s'allonge à mesure que le vent et la poussière nous blanchissent la vie!

Imaginez donc! Au cœur de ce désert, un pont par lequel tous les voyageurs doivent passer! Et qu'est-ce qu'on y trouve? Un péage! C'est un tournant pour toute personne allant vers Kousseri. Un péage! « Tout le monde paie », est-il écrit. Des militaires, armes aux poings, reçoivent la recette. Après le pont et son péage, le désert continue sa chanson et le Sahel siffle. En roulant, on a l'impression d'aller vers la fin du monde.

Nous arrivons à Kousséri au crépuscule. C'est plus une ville tchadienne que camerounaise. Un moto-taximan me conduit à Nguéli. Je sais déjà, malgré la libre circulation CEMAC dont parlent les médias, qu'il faut payer, payer à chaque fois. J'ai préparé depuis Yaoundé, une série de billets de 1 000 FCFA pour les contrôles à l'entrée de N'Djaména. Je sais qu'on paye 500 FCFA, mais mon passeport dit que je suis un « écrivain ». Pour les contrôleurs, cela veut dire que j'ai beaucoup d'argent – donc, je paye le double. À chaque poste, lorsqu'il faut payer une somme, je paye le double. Surtout, ne pas se plaindre, ne rien dire. Sinon, on envoie votre passeport chez le « Chef ».

Dans les aéroports, lorsqu'on me remet mon passeport, c'est toujours avec un sourire. L'agent vous fait un commentaire rapide sur un livre qu'il a lu quand il était à l'école primaire, l'autre demande si vos œuvres sont inscrites au programme scolaire.

Parfois, un policier vous avoue qu'il écrit des poèmes! D'autres vous citent quelques auteurs. Ici, à la frontière, il faut juste payer. Payer le double.

Contributors

Howard M-B Maximus is a staff writer at Bakwa. In 2017 he participated in the Goethe-Institut Literary Exchange Programme, and in 2018 he was shortlisted for the Miles Morland Writing Scholarship. His work has featured in *Catapult* and *The Africa Report* among other places. He is working on a novel and short story collection.

Yovanka Paquete Perdigao is a Bissau-Guinean writer, editor, and translator. Born in Lisbon, she grew up in Guinea-Bissau until the age of six when a civil war in 1998 forced her and her family to return to Lisbon as refugees, and she has since lived in Ivory Coast, Senegal, and now London. Yovanka's writing has been featured in several platforms such as *Brittle Paper*, *AFREADA*, and *Ozy*. She was longlisted for Penguin 2016 WriteNow, and her short fiction "Crying Cobalt Blue" was highly commended for the Spread the Word's City of Stories competition. She is Assistant Editor at Dedalus Books and former co-host of the Not Another Book Podcast as PostcolonialChild.

Kay Ugwuede is a nonfiction writer and freelance journalist based in Lagos, Nigeria. Her work cuts across culture, governance, and the dynamics of belief systems. She has been published in *CityLab*, *BusinessDay*, *Kalahari Review*, and *Aerodrome*, among other places. Email: kugwuede@gmail.com

Munukayumbwa 'Mimi' Mwiya is a floater who sometimes sits still long enough to write. She is Namibian.

Sada Malumfashi lives in Kaduna, Nigeria. His fiction has appeared in *Transition* and *New Orleans Review*'s The African Literary Hustle issue. His essays and creative nonfiction have appeared or are forthcoming in *The Africa Report*, *Saraba*, *Enkare Review*, *This Is Africa*, and *Music in Africa*, among other venues. He participated in the Goethe-Institut Nigeria-Cameroon Literary Exchange Programme and is an awardee of the Goethe Institut-Sylt Foundation Writing Residency through the Literary Exchange Program. He is interested in the intricacies of languages and works bilingually on translations between Hausa and English. His poem and translations from the Hausa have appeared in the National Translation Month issue of *2017*.

Nkiacha Atemnkeng is a Cameroonian writer who works at the Douala International Airport. His works have been published in the Caine Prize anthology, 'Lusaka Punk and Other Stories,' The Africa Report, Culture Trip, This Is Africa, Bakwa, Saraba and Gyara Magazines. He attended the 2015 Caine Prize writer's workshop in Ghana, the 2017 Nigeria Cameroon Literary Exchange Project and the 2018 Miles Morland workshop in Uganda, facilitated by Giles Foden. He is a Sylt Foundation writing residency prize winner and was invited to the Writer's Omi and Kundslerdorf Schoppingen residencies. He is currently working on a manuscript set at the Douala Airport, the city of Douala and two western airports, tentatively titled *Gate A-22*. He tweets @nkiacha

Anne Marie Befoune est Camerounaise, traductrice de formation, mais sa passion pour l'action citoyenne l'a poussée à en faire un combat d'un côté et un métier de l'autre. Elle écrit des articles socio-politiques pour divers média internationaux.

Ecrivain et blogueur camerounais, **Florian Ngimbis** s'est fait remarquer en remportant le Prix du Jeune Ecrivain de langue Française 2008. Ses nouvelles ont été publiées dans plusieurs recueils et revues littéraires. Son blog Kamer Kongossa dépeint au vitriol mais avec humour le Cameroun contemporain. Il a été primé en 2012 lors des prestigieux Deutsche Welle Blogs Awards (The Bob's) dans la catégorie « Meilleur Blog Francophone ».

Raoul Djimeli est écrivain et activiste culturel. Au Cameroun, il dirige la publication du magazine littéraire *Clijec Mag'* et préside *l'African Festival of Emerging Writings* (Festae). Ses poèmes et sa prose sont parus en français, en anglais et traduits en Kiswahili et en espagnol, dans divers collectifs et revues, y compris l'anthologie intercontinentale *Oír ese Río*, parue en Colombie. Il a participé au *Limbe-Lagos Literary Exchange Programme* initié par les magazines africains, Bakwa et Saraba avec le soutien de l'Institut Goethe, et au premier projet de fictions Afro Young Adult dont l'anthologie, *Water Birds on the Lakeshore* paraît en octobre chez Ouida Books au Nigeria. Raoul Djimeli a codirigé le projet poétique *Ashes and Memories* sur la crise anglophone au Cameroun. Deux fois lauréat du prix *Poésie en liberté*, ses écrits ont également été récompensés en Côte d'Ivoire et au Cameroun. Son recueil de poèmes, *Le Front brûlant de l'aube*, est paru en juillet 2019 chez Les bruits de l'encre, à Bafoussam.

Sign up for our newsletter at www.bakwamagazine.com and receive exclusive updates, including extracts, podcasts, event notifications, discounts, competitions and giveaways.

Follow Bakwa Magazine

Twitter: @BakwaMag

Instagram: @Bakwa_Magazine

Facebook: Bakwa Magazine

www.ingramcontent.com/pod-product-compliance
Lightning Source LLC
Chambersburg PA
CBHW011957150426
43200CB00018B/2934